"Every child of God longs to have a close, 'Abba-Daddy' relationship with the heavenly Father. With personal transparency and biblical encouragement, Debi Newman picks up where the pulpit stops. She gently guides us on an intimate journey to the Father's heart—and helps us to understand clearly how we can truly experience that kind of relationship for ourselves."

Rebecca Barlow Jordan, best-selling author,
Daily in Your Presence

"Dr. Deborah Newman is a leading evangelical expert on the subject of relationships. Dr. Newman suggests everyday life is affected by the interpersonal scripts we have adopted. The same holds true on the spiritual level as well in that our view of our heavenly Father is often developed from a portrait we have etched in our minds of our earthly father.

"In her book, Dr. Newman provides creative yet profound and practical ways to see God and communicate with Him in a realistic manner, void of erroneous, airbrushed conceptions that have been the cause of many a confusion.

"This book will help the reader see God in a new, fresh, and intimate way . . . the prerequisite for having a meaningful prayer life with Him!"

Dr. Rick Fowler, author, *Too Busy to Live*; executive director,
Prestonwood Counseling Centers

"All of us as humans see God through eyes that are prejudiced by our past experiences. We tend to think, *Dear heavenly version of my earthly father*. But Dr. Newman guides us here to see and experience real intimacy with the real God."

Paul Meier. M.D.. author: founder, Meier Clinics

D1114300

"When we recognize God as 'Abba Father' we draw close to Him in a deeper, more secure relationship. Debi Newman invites us to make a breakthrough in our relationship with God by going beyond simply seeing God as our friend to embracing Him as our loving Father. Her book broadens our understanding and beckons us to run into God's loving arms."

Karol Ladd, best-selling author, speaker

"I have been a fan of Dr. Deborah Newman since I met her in the early 1990s. She has always amazed me with her keen insight, wisdom, and ability to connect with those who feel alienated. In *How to Love God as Your Father* she helps all of us make the most important connection of all with God and shows us how to love our heavenly Father, even if our earthly father wasn't too heavenly. This will be a breakthrough book for many readers."

Stephen Arterburn, founder, New Life Ministries

"Foundational, inspirational, different, practicable, vulnerable, warm—these are only a few of the adjectives that describe the galvanizing concept Dr. Deborah Newman holds forth; with perspicacity and astute applications she elucidates a dream that can come true for Christians in a beautiful and intimate relationship with God; this book is a rare jewel."

Frank Minirth, M.D., Ph.D., author, *Happiness Is a Choice*

"I have known so many believers who struggle with the 'father-image' of God and don't really know what it means to truly trust Him as Jesus did even in the days of the cross. But Dr. Newman's book makes us want to turn and embrace Him as Father—even as He embraces us as His children."

Rev. Canon David H. Roseberry, Christ Church, Plano, Texas

How to Really Love God as Your Father

Growing Your Most Important Relationship

Dr. Deborah Newman

BakerBooks
Grand Rapids, Michigan

© 2005 by Deborah Newman

Published by Baker Books
a division of Baker Publishing Group
P.O. Box 6287, Grand Rapids, MI 49516-6287
www.bakerbooks.com

Printed in the United States of America

Library of Congress Cataloging-in-Publication Data
Newman, Deborah.
    How to really love God as your father : growing your most important relationship / Deborah Newman.
         p.   cm.
    Includes bibliographical references.
    ISBN 0-8010-6537-2 (pbk.)
    1. God—Fatherhood. I. Title.
BT153.F3N49 2005
231'.1—dc22   2005012321

The case examples presented in this book are fictional composites based on the author's clinical experience with hundreds of individuals through the years. Any resemblance between these fictional characters and actual persons is coincidental.

With gratitude to Bob and Norma Bowles,
my earthly parents, who introduced me
to my heavenly Father

Contents

Acknowledgments

I'm not sure how I was so fortunate to be chosen to write this book. I thank God for inspiring me and making a way for this book to be published. I pray that it honors Him in every way.

I'm more than grateful to my husband, research assistant, life partner, and friend. Brian is very much my collaborator in writing this book by giving me all the time, encouragement, and help that I needed. Rachel and Ben, you provide great stories and teach me so much about life.

This book was read in its early stages by friends in a writers workshop: Mondrell Oz, Diane Walker, Charlotte Lynas, and Anna Imgrund. Later, Janet Denison, Cinde Rawn, and Steve Ingino offered me a great gift by reading and commenting on the manuscript. Each gave me unique insights that were incorporated into what I wrote.

I'm grateful to Jeremy Copeland, Lois Ward, Carol Scott, and Verdell Krisher, who granted me permission to share their examples.

My readers at www.TeaTimeForYourSoul.com helped me suggest the title.

Karol Ladd dreamed and prayed with me about this project from the beginning.

You wouldn't be reading this book today if Bob Hosack and Baker Books didn't have a vision for it. Thank you, Bob, for thinking this would be a worthy project for Baker to undertake. I'm grateful to Kristin Kornoelje for her perceptive editing, and to the rest of the Baker Team. I may never know them by name, but I do appreciate their contribution.

Finally, I thank you for reading the book and pray that God will use it in your life for His glory.

Foreword

Father—that word stirs many different thoughts, emotions, and memories for each one of us. How you and I relate to God the Father depends on many different life experiences—one being the relationship with our own earthly father. Every person has a father, known or unknown, close or distant, loving or rejecting. To come to God the Father can be warm and welcoming as well as frightening and challenging.

I pray that as you read this book, God will become the heavenly Father you long for. I pray that your misunderstandings, misperceptions, misappropriations will be melted away by the realization that God stubbornly loves you and gave you the gift of His very own Son in order to be in a relationship with you.

As you begin this adventure of faith, excitement, and communion with the one true God, allow the forgiveness and freedom of Christ to guide your heart and mind to His Father. Invite the power of the Holy Spirit to guard your heart and mind and to fill you full of the awareness that you are God's beloved son or daughter. And may you experience in a new and fresh way the unconditional love of our Father God.

Dr. Brian Newman, Minister of Education,
Park Cities Baptist Church,
Dallas, 2005

Part 1

The God You Can Know as "Daddy"

1 You Can Call God "Daddy"

"Abba, Father," he said, "everything is possible for you. Take this cup from me. Yet not what I will, but what you will."

Mark 14:36

Some of you know what I'm talking about when I say, "You can call God 'Daddy.'" You've personally experienced prayer that feels like falling into the arms of your Father. You know what cuddling up to the God who invites you to call Him Daddy feels like. You've been empowered, inspired, and humbled by realizing your Abba-Father, Daddy-God is there for you. It's an experience you want to understand better and to live more. Or you may feel your soul is searching for deeper intimacy with God, and you have picked up this book in hopes of discovering how to make that connection. You may be so baffled by the word "Daddy" that you find associating this term with God to be complicated and difficult. I guarantee you that if you learn to claim your identity as "Abba's child," it will dramatically impact your life; you might even develop a whole new connotation for the word "Daddy" in reference to God.

Through the years of my spiritual journey, I have bumped into Scriptures that have stunned and amazed me. The first was in the Gospel of Mark, when Jesus prayed to God as "Abba," or "Daddy" in English (Mark 14:36). The realization that I can call God "Daddy" is a result of what I read in Romans 8:14–17, 23; Galatians 3:26; 4:6; and Ephesians 1:4–5. In this book you are invited to settle in and cuddle up to the God who invites you to call Him "Daddy."

I actually thought about not using the word "Daddy" in this book, although it is the best English translation of "Abba." So many people have told me that this word is foreign to them even in their human family relationships. Jesus is trying to teach us that really knowing God is more than knowing Him as Father; it is actually knowing Him as "Daddy" (or Dad, Papa, Pop). As you read, please insert the name for father that signifies the closest intimacy you can imagine from a paternal figure. I pray that you will grow to love this name for God even though you may never know an earthly father as "Daddy."

I also need to state that our God is worthy of honor and glory. This book examines only one facet of the infinite nature of God. God is the Creator. He is holy. He is omnipotent. He is the King of Kings and Lord of Lords. He is all that and more, and still He invites you to cry out "Abba" when you address Him. This book seeks only to understand the mystery of what it means to call God "Daddy." It is not an exhaustive study of God and doesn't even begin to examine His full nature.

When I first read the Scriptures that told me to call God "Daddy," I couldn't even come close to comprehending what they meant. What began as abstract knowledge slowly took form and created an intimate connection to God. It happened in much the same way erosion shapes stone. Like water dripping slowly and consistently, a calm and transforming presence broke through the hard places in my soul that had never imagined God could love me like a daddy. I have a strong feeling that many other Christians have never fully comprehended that praying is actually talking to our Dad.

I enjoyed reading the biography of Samuel Morris. He was born a prince of his tribe in the African country of Liberia. After his conversion by Methodist missionaries, he eventually journeyed to America, not as a slave but as a short-term missionary urging Americans to go tell those in other countries about Jesus. Morris learned to pray from watching others. He came to the conclusion that prayer was talking to his Father. His biographer writes, "To his childlike faith, prayer was [as] simple and as sure as conversing with an earthly parent."[1]

How I wish I had understood prayer this way for my entire Christian life! Only in the last ten years have I come to taste the true power and intimacy of prayer. Samuel Morris had an advantage in that he intuitively understood how to have a dual relationship with a father who was also a ruler: he was the son of a chief. Although his father was the chief of his tribe, he was also Samuel's loving parent. Samuel Morris transferred this understanding to his relationship with God. He always perceived prayer as talking to his dad.

Jesus's death and resurrection created the potential for us to have a whole new relationship with God that was never possible before. When Jesus died on the cross, the curtain in the temple in Jerusalem tore from top to bottom. Since the time of Moses, people had to be kept at a distance from God. God prescribed this curtain so even the priests would not look inside the Holy of Holies, where God lived among His people. It is extremely significant that this curtain tore as Jesus hung dying on the cross. It was God's invitation to us to come closer through the blood of Christ. The Holy of Holies (the place God dwelt) was exposed to man. I'm hoping that you are able to grasp the fact that before Jesus, no one dared consider attributing the kind of intimacy a name like "Daddy" implies to a holy God. Yet the love of our "Daddy" is just what Jesus wants us to grasp.

The most remarkable result of coming to know God as "Abba-Daddy" in my life is that I have begun to grasp who I really am. Knowing God as Dad has given me the strength I need to face my problems, even when God doesn't solve them for me or take them away. When you learn to pray to God as Father, you will see yourself as God's child too. He will stand you before the mirror of your soul and reveal your true identity. Something will radically change in the deepest recesses of your spiritual self when you learn to call Him "Daddy."

Henri Nouwen describes it this way: "Calling God 'Abba' is entering into the same intimate, fearless, trusting, and empowering relationship with God that Jesus had. That relationship is called Spirit, and that Spirit is given to us by Jesus and enables us to cry out with him, 'Abba, Father.' . . . It has nothing to do with naming God but everything to do with claiming God as the source of who we are."[2] Calling God "Daddy" can be the most empowering experience of your spiritual life.

What happened in my prayer life reminds me of a memory I have from fifth grade. That year my church opened a Christian school and my siblings and I were some of its first students. Not only was my school brand new, but my teacher was a first-year novice who was unprepared for the lack of support and the extreme challenge presented by a room of insecure fifth graders. In my former school I had been the "good girl," but something about the lack of structure in the classroom and my preadolescence collided, and I began to enjoy the little disruptions I could get away with in the classroom. I preferred hanging out with a like-minded circle who encouraged my drift into delinquency. The day my novice teacher cussed at our class and left the room in tears was the beginning of big changes in my life. She decided to resign, and Mrs. Nagle took her place. From the moment Mrs.

Nagel took over our classroom, my behavior took a turn for the better.

I experienced an encounter with Mrs. Nagel that is similar to what has happened in my relationship with God. The encounter occurred in the girls' restroom when Mrs. Nagel walked in and caught me off guard in a tearful moment. I can't recall why I was crying, but I know I was as upset as a fifth-grade girl could be about a fifth-grade problem. One of the things I do remember, though, was feeling that I didn't care to talk about my problem with Mrs. Nagel. I was upset that she intruded on my private moment of tearful release, but that didn't stop her. She ignored any disdain I sent her way and kept pursuing me in my pain. I'm not sure if I told her what was bothering me. In fact, I think I remained true to my self-protection and didn't reveal the reason for my tears. But my encounter with Mrs. Nagel changed how I saw myself.

The most memorable part of the exchange was when she put her hands on my shoulders and walked me over to the mirror. She told me to look in the mirror. She said, "You see that girl? She is a strong, beautiful, wonderful girl. Now give me a smile." Deep inside, I wanted to resist. After all, she didn't solve my problem; I still had something going on in my life that made me sad enough to risk tears in the girls' restroom. I smiled anyway.

Between that moment and my graduation to sixth grade I became a different girl. That moment of love, care, and encouragement affected something inside me. I wanted to be better. I believed I was better. I never imagined that I could feel that close and that valuable to my fifth-grade teacher. It took much longer for me to realize just how important I am to God.

What Happens When You Pray?

Do you wake up each morning with the thought that you are loved by God in the forefront of your mind? Do you enter your day wondering what ways God will show you more of His love for you and His purpose for your life? Are you excited about the many opportunities a new day will bring to glorify God? Is your only concern that you have a limited number of days on this earth to serve Him?

Probably not. But wouldn't it be nice, just once, to wake up with that much enthusiasm for God and for life? The reason for our lack of enthusiasm for prayer is found by answering two questions: "How do you see God when you pray?" and "How do you see yourself after you pray?"

How Do You See God When You Pray?

Do you approach God in the assurance that He loves you like a daddy loves his child? Do you know without a doubt that you are always wanted, even when you are broken and ashamed? Have you ever approached God knowing full well the reality of your utter poverty and received a compassion-filled kiss and embrace? When you have, you will find yourself with a deep desire to pray more.

I was a Christian for many years before I learned how to pray to God as "Daddy." I had prayed a lot of prayers. But my prayer life took off to new levels of intimacy and intensity when I let God embrace me in the same way a good daddy embraces his child.

Brennan Manning tells this story: A priest visited his uncle in Ireland on his eightieth birthday. The special day began with an early morning walk to observe the sunrise. The two had shared a long morning of quiet, but a curious look on his uncle's face demanded the priest ask a question. Impressed, the priest said, "Uncle Seamus, you really look happy." "I am, lad." "Want to tell me why?" His eighty-year-old uncle replied, "Yes, you see, me Abba is very fond of me."[3] Do you know that God is very fond of you (1 John 3:1)? Do you call him "Abba"?

Once I began to realize the closeness possible in prayer, I began to want to come to God for comforting, helpful, important conversation. Sadly, many miss out on this kind of intimacy. Many Christians don't know what being embraced by God in prayer means simply because they need to be told it is possible. They need to experience the healing force of praying to God as their Father. Prayerlessness pervades our world because most Christians don't really know God as Father. If we really understood that prayer is an encounter with a wise, loving, nurturing Daddy, we would do a lot more of it.

How Do You See Yourself after You Pray?

When I see God as Abba, I can't help but come face-to-face with the fact that I am Abba's child. When I see myself this way, I understand my purpose and importance in a whole new light. As I have reflected back on my journey with God, I have recognized a cycle that has brought me to this feeling of intimacy with Him. This cycle became the basis of this book. I hope to share how God has become my "Daddy" so that you will be able to understand how you can have this same experience with Him. As you read, you may recognize similar experiences along your spiritual journey. The cycle looks like this.

Cycle of Intimacy with God

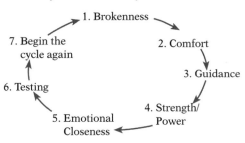

In part 2 of this book I explain this cycle of intimacy with God. But first I want to explore some foundational truths about God that I hope will stir your senses and your yearning to belong intimately to God. In this chapter we will explore the fact that God desires you to think of Him as your Father. Chapter 2 will expose the truth that you must consider how your bond to your earthly father (or parents, or father figures) affects your relationship with your heavenly Father. The third chapter will help you realize that God is a Father who wants to dote on you. He wants to give you so much, if you are willing to accept it.

God Desires for You to Know Him as Your Father

Praying to God as Father was as natural to Jesus as breathing. His entire identity rested in the truth that He was the Son of God. Read John's Gospel and note the constant focus on God as Jesus's Father. Jesus told us that He did only what He saw His Father doing (John 5:19). His existence on Earth was His Father's idea (John 1:14). His purpose in coming was to make the Father known to us (John 1:18). He knew that in relationship with His Father He had everything He could possibly want (John 3:35; 5:20).

Jesus showed us more about what kind of Father we can know than about any other attribute of God. Jesus rarely called God anything other than Father. Every day Jesus demonstrated what it is like to live on Earth with a close connection to a heavenly Father and know Him well enough to call Him "Daddy-God."

As the disciples spent time with Jesus, they observed Him praying on many occasions. Every time Jesus had a free moment (and at times He would sacrifice a meal or other opportunities to make a free moment), He seemed to want to get away to enjoy God in prayer. When the disciples observed Jesus's passion for prayer, they may have wondered, *What are we missing out on? The thought of prayer doesn't seem to compel us the way it does Jesus.* The disciples sensed that something amazing was happening when Jesus prayed. They wanted to experience it for themselves, so they asked Jesus to teach them to pray (Luke 11:1).

The first two words of the prayer Jesus taught the disciples in response to their request were "Our Father." Jesus didn't pray "My Father." Unbelievable as it may sound, Jesus's answer to their question was an invitation to know God as Father the way Jesus did.

On the eve of His crucifixion, Jesus further revealed to the disciples that God is the kind of Father they could call Daddy. The disciples were not surprised that Jesus would want to pray in the Garden of Gethsemane after they celebrated the Passover dinner together. Although a lot of things Jesus said and did confused them that night (such as washing the disciples' feet, telling them that one among them would betray Him, and predicting Peter's denials), this prayer time did not surprise them at all. The path to prayer was well worn; Judas knew about it and was confident he could lead the priests to Jesus there.

The disciples sat while Jesus prayed, not even aware of the spiritual battles that were taking place. Jesus invited Peter, James, and John to come closer and to watch with Him in prayer. These spiritual leaders of the group couldn't keep their eyes open and dosed off while Jesus prayed.

Although everyone else was oblivious, one Gospel writer recorded the exact wording of Jesus's world-changing prayer. Mark may have overheard this prayer himself. Some believe that the Gospel of Mark was written by John Mark, who may have been the same young man who ran away naked from the Garden on the night of Jesus's arrest (Mark 14:51–52). Although we cannot know for certain if he overheard Jesus's prayer himself, Mark's Gospel gives witness to the word Jesus used that night to address His Father in this monumental prayer:

"Abba, Father," he said, "everything is possible for you. Take this cup from me. Yet not what I will, but what you will."

Mark 14:36

This simple prayer, these heartfelt words, and the intimacy they expressed are what transformed Jesus from one so troubled in spirit He was sweating drops of blood (Luke 22:44) to the one who courageously embraced the most dreadful reality possible: paying for all of mankind's sins with His very life.

Jesus Taught Us to Pray to Our Abba-Father, Daddy-God

First and foremost, Jesus came to solve the problem of sin for people who are infinitely loved by a holy God. Sin could be dealt with only one way, and that was for Jesus to be the sinless sacrifice. If you accept Jesus as your Savior, you can be reconciled in your relationship with God and know Him as your Father (Rom. 10:9–10).

Jesus's death made it possible for you to know God. Jesus opened the windows of our souls to the breeze of heaven. He shows us how to see God as Father and then as "Daddy." God produced a literal picture of Jesus unveiling God to us when, just as Jesus died, the temple veil tore in two and exposed the Holy of Holies, the place God dwelt (Matt. 27:50–51).

Jesus was aware that the Pharisees, disciples, and followers had knowledge of God. To them God was Elohiym, Yahweh, and the Great I Am. They were aware that God existed and had revealed Himself through certain prophets who relayed God's words to man. Many of them knew God's Word and had committed it to memory and studied it for years. Yet in all their efforts to know God, somehow they missed His true character.

Jesus was the living Word of God, His whole existence a deeper revelation of who God is (John 1:14, 18). Jesus told His disciples that if they had seen Him, they had seen the Father (John 14:9). The aspect of who God is that most empowered Jesus's life was that God was and would always remain His Father, the kind of Father He felt comfortable calling "Daddy."

What Do You Call Your Father?

If you were raised in the southern U.S., you will most likely make reference to your father as "Daddy" whether he was kind, distant, or a violent alcoholic. Using the word "Daddy" to refer to your paternal parent has a cultural element to it. If your answer to "What do you call your father?" is "Daddy," that is no guarantee that you understand what was reflected in Jesus's use of the term "Daddy" to describe His relationship with His Father. Calling God "Daddy" is more than semantics; it's about a vibrant, intimate relationship.

As you grew up, did you see your dad as a man of love? Did you get the sense from him that nothing you could ever do would stop him from loving you? Did you know beyond a shadow of a doubt that you could disappoint or hurt him, but you could never do anything that would cause him not to love you? Nothing can separate you from the love of a daddy! Nothing can separate you from the love of God (Rom. 8:39)!

Helping us understand that kind of Daddy-love was a difficult task for Jesus. One way Jesus showed us God's Daddy-love was when He told the parable of the prodigal son (Luke 15:11–32). This tale has grown familiar to us, but the story was totally shocking to Hebrew ears. Jesus told about a father who had two sons. The younger son came to his father and lamented, "I wish I could have my inheritance now and not have to wait until you die to have my fun!" By asking for his inheritance, the son was in essence saying, "I wish you were dead, because the only thing standing between me and my inheritance is that you are

25

still alive." No father in his right mind would consider a request like that, would he?

Keep in mind that the father in this parable represents God. Jesus used this story to convey that God's fatherly love far exceeds typical human standards. The parable expresses the lostness of humanity and God's desperate desire to bring His children home and hold them close. Like the father in this story, God cares more about reconciling with His children than about anything He owns or possesses.

After the greedy son was given his inheritance, he didn't wait long to hit the road, showing little concern for his father's feelings. He traveled to a distant land and lived without restraint. He completely ignored the values of the home in which he was brought up. As long as he had money, he had friends, women, and food galore; but when it was all gone, he was alone and hungry. You'll remember that this high-born Hebrew found himself feeding pigs, animals detested by Jews. He really hit bottom when he realized that he longed for the food he fed the pigs. How much lower can you get than that?

At that point he began to think about his father's home again. He remembered that his father's servants didn't feed pigs and were treated pretty well in comparison to his present situation. So he decided it was worth trying to get his father to take him on as a servant in his household. He planned a humble speech and hoped for the good graces of the man he had once known as Dad. He could never have prepared himself for what he experienced.

When he was still far down the lane to home, mustering up all the optimism he could to face his father again, his father saw him and ran to meet him. Before the son could even finish his speech asking for a job as a servant, his father had embraced him, kissed him, and ordered the servants to make his lost son welcome with clothes, rings, and a feast fit for a son who had done something amazing.

Who has ever heard of a father like that? All the son did was come home. He didn't earn a degree, land a great job, get married, have a child—any of the reasons you might think a father would be proud enough to throw a party. All he did was come home with nothing to offer. It didn't seem fair, especially to the father's older son, who felt angry, jealous, and wounded by his father's demonstration of love.

You've observed loving parents; you know about forgiving parents; you may see caring parents every day. How often do you witness a father giving this kind of love to one so undeserving? He is overflowing in compassion for a son who has ignored and mistreated him.

That kind of love—irrational from a human perspective—is what Jesus was depicting when He told the story of the prodigal son. Through the story Jesus showed us how much God loves us—however we respond to Him as Father. If we are the prodigal son who leaves the father, barely acknowledging his existence and behaving in a way that he disapproves of, the father never stops loving, watching, and longing for the child he loves. If we obey him out of duty, like the older brother, and misunderstand his heart and who he is, he will still come out to us, reveal who he is, and attempt to bring us in.

Jesus used this story to convey a message to a bunch of hard-hearted listeners. Truthfully, most of them didn't understand. They didn't recognize that they were the older brother, judging the father's love as ridiculous. Jesus wanted to open their hearts to the irrational love of their heavenly Father, but most of them remained closed. I wonder what will happen to your heart as you look deeper into what it means that God is your Father. Will you remain hard-hearted and distant, judging God's goodness as wrong and irrational, or will you believe and enjoy His love?

Perhaps your own father fell short as a daddy, not even close to the example in Jesus's parable, as many fathers do. At times you may have believed your dad didn't care about you at all; he may have been a poor example of a Christian or been completely absent from your life. You could be letting your earthly experience keep you from knowing the fatherly love of God. You are His child and you mean so much to Him. He wants to show you your worth. But first you must believe that knowing God as your Daddy is worthwhile.

The ideal daddy conjures up a sense of undeniable love, wisdom, caring, and provision. A dad was meant to be all that to you. Having had a negative experience with your father can block you from taking in the full nature of the relationship God offers you. We can't move further in experiencing how to love God as Father without first visiting your feelings about your earthly parents and parent figures.

Reflection Questions:

1. Why did God invite us to call Him "Abba-Father, Daddy-God"?
2. When did you first comprehend that God wants you to feel as close to Him as a dad?
3. What keeps you from responding to His invitation to know Him as your Daddy?
4. What kind of child of God are you more like—the prodigal or the elder son?
5. What experiences have you had with God in which He felt like a "Daddy"?
6. Write a letter to God addressing Him as "Daddy," and tell Him the concerns that are on your heart. Read Scripture and write down what He says back to you.

Intimacy Exercise:

Draw, describe, or imagine what a good dad would be like. What would he talk about? How would he interact with you? What might he want to do for his child? What characteristics or qualities make a good dad? What is a good dad like?

2 The Orphaned Soul

I will not leave you as orphans, I will come to you.

John 14:18

I hope that reading the first chapter of this book has inspired you to want to really love God as your Father. The whole concept that God holds you in the same esteem as a proud father does his own child can be enticing yet difficult to embrace. Knowing it in your head is not enough. Something must radically change inside of you before you can really know God this way. Praying to God as Abba, Daddy, cannot be experienced without a deep and secure trust. You must have a spiritual breakthrough, understanding that God is a perfect Father, unlike any you have ever known.

E. M. Bounds was a man who really knew God as Father. He spent a minimum of three hours a day in prayer.[1] No one in his right mind voluntarily spends three hours a day doing something that has little benefit to them. So what benefit kept this man so passionate about prayer? We gain insight to what his answer might have been by the way he described prayer: "Prayer is the contact of a living soul with God. In prayer God stoops to kiss man, to bless man and to aid in everything that God can devise or man can need."[2]

Now, let me ask you, would you describe your relationship with God like that? Do you feel that God is actually touching your soul when you pray? Do you sense God stooping from heaven to kiss you, bless you, and help you with your every need? Do you see yourself as one of God's constant preoccupations?

Are you ready to let your heart accept the love God desires to give you? No father on Earth has ever been able to compare to the way God loves you as your Father. To understand praying to God as Father we must unpack why seeing Him as Father is so hard. The impact of your earthly father on your relationship with God is huge. You may never be able to embrace God as your Father until you let go of your notion of what a father is.

A friend of mine worked one summer for a Christian organization ministering to children in the inner city of Chicago. She was instructed not to use the word "father" to describe God to the kids she was trying to reach. She was told most of the kids didn't even know who their father was, had been abandoned by him, or had a father who was in jail. Instead, she was to describe God as a "best friend." That was a concept they could understand.

I'm inviting you to make a breakthrough—to go beyond thinking of God as your friend. Rather, I hope you will go deep enough to really know God as your Father and, deeper still, your Daddy. Broadening your concept of God as your Daddy begins when you make a conscious decision to transfer your love and loyalty from earthly parents to God.

Parent-Child Loyalties Run Deep

We have a natural loyalty to our earthly parents, whether they were good or bad. This bond is hard to break on both sides.

From the moment I first held my daughter (my firstborn), I have been amazed at the connection and deep love I have for her. The instant they laid her in my arms, I discovered a new level of love for another human being, one I had never felt before. Recently I was out of town on a speaking engagement but able to keep connected to home through the Internet. I used a dial-up service to get online, and everything was working fine. Earlier I had written my daughter, now a teenager, and I saw that she had responded to my email. I had received other business emails that I needed to answer, and I was saving her email until last. Just as I was about to open hers, out of nowhere I was bumped from my connection to the Internet. I couldn't believe it. I tried to reconnect. The same thing happened. I tried multiple times. I kept trying and praying, all the while knowing that the message didn't contain news that was vital for me to read at that moment. If it had been any other email—sent from anyone else but one of my children—I would have tried a few times and given up, resolved to wait until later. But an email from my sixteen-year-old daughter caused me to try again and again.

The connection from child to parent is just as strong. This connection can be a negative connection, a positive connection, or a little of both. Spiritual maturity involves transferring our parenting connection from our earthly parents to God. The sad truth is that some never make that transfer, even long after their earthly parents are gone.

During my eighteen years as a Christian counselor, I met hundreds of people who dealt with unresolved pain from their relationship with their parents. Many were not even aware that their emotional problems were somehow connected to their relationship with their parents. Linda is an interesting example. She called my secretary two days before her second appointment with me. She had a strange request. She asked my secretary if she could remove a statue that sat on a bookcase in my office before her 11:15 a.m. appointment and return it afterward. My secretary didn't know how to answer a question like that and told Linda that she would have to talk to me about it.

The statue that Linda wanted removed was a tender scene of a father holding his little girl in his arms. Just thinking about seeing it again touched off deep feelings inside Linda that she wasn't ready to deal with.

You never would have guessed how negative her feelings about her dad were by the way she lived her life. Linda had four siblings, but she was the one who offered the major care for her nursing-home-bound father. The aversion she had toward him was never evident in her behavior.

Through several months of counseling, Linda learned how to deal with those feelings. I felt greatly rewarded to watch her experience the freedom of forgiving her father. Near the end of her counseling, Linda discovered that a major spiritual block in her relationship with God was the feeling of rejection from her dad that she had unknowingly transferred onto God. She found out that she couldn't really connect to God until she healed from the rejection of her earthly father.

When You Have a Negative Connection

How have you felt as I have mentioned the word *daddy* so often in reference to God? Is *daddy* a dirty word in your subconscious? You may be one of those who are having a hard time connecting to the English word *daddy* that translates from the Aramaic word *Abba*. You may have even thought about putting this book down a time or two just because the word stings your psyche. For you a daddy may be someone who has caused deep regret in your life.

Perhaps the way your father mistreated you is the reason you doubt you are worthy of God's love. When children are abused they often think, *If my own dad could do that to me, then there must be something wrong with me.* If your earthly father mistreated you, then you have an even greater need to learn how to pray to God as Daddy. Your Abba-Father, Daddy-God is particularly concerned with your wounds and your need for His love. Your soul has always wanted but never come close to receiving the love that is offered to you. You may have lost hope that the pain from your relationship with your earthly father could be fully healed through a heavenly Daddy's touch.

Emotional Orphans

Many people are walking around the planet as emotional orphans. They wouldn't identify themselves with this label, but if they stopped long enough to examine the motivation behind their behavior, they would see that much of it is an attempt to fill needs for love that their parents wouldn't or couldn't meet. Acknowledging their orphaned state and healing it through forgiveness opens the door to loving God as Father. Parents hurt their children. Some of them do so without purposely setting out to cause harm. In fact, often the most hurtful things parents do are out of a desire to protect their children—yet they still cause pain.

All of us need to practice forgiveness in every relationship of our lives. It is especially important in our relationship with our parents. They are the two people we hold most accountable to love and care for us. When they fail us in any way, that impacts how we see ourselves, our world, and especially God. In order to honestly open our hearts to God as our Father, we need to remove the obstacles set up by unforgiveness of our earthly parents.

Gary's dad was the spiritual leader of his home. He took Gary and his brothers and sisters to church every week. Gary's mom was sick with multiple sclerosis and could do little to help the family. The pressure Gary's father felt from working, raising a family, and caring for a sick wife would often come out in rage directed at Gary. Being the firstborn, Gary tried to help his dad out, but his help was rarely recognized. When Gary forgot to do something or made a mistake were the only times he received his father's attention—and his rage. Gary was definitely physically abused, but not in a way that outsiders could notice. The bruises were well covered; even Gary took extra precautions to protect his father's secret.

Deep down Gary believed that he deserved the beatings. He both hated and loved his father. As an adult, he tried not to think about his childhood, convincing himself that everything was over now. He had survived, and that was all he needed to know. Gary's mother had died, and his father now lived with Gary's youngest sister. Gary believed the past was the past and proved it by never laying a hand on either of his two children. He found other ways of discipline. Only when Gary sought a deeper relationship with God did the reality of his father's abuse become a boundary that kept him from opening his heart to God as he wanted. Praying to Daddy is not a comfortable thought for most men. For Gary it was repulsive. The only active parent he knew was his dad, and all he had ever received from him was disapproval.

One day his mentor asked him to visualize God when he prayed and to share the image he saw of God. Gary was shocked to admit that when he thought of praying before God, he saw himself hiding behind a curtain and shouting up to a mean and angry man sitting on a throne with rage in his eyes. Gary's mentor asked him who that angry man was. For the first time Gary realized that he had placed the characteristics of his earthly father on the God he was trying to get close to.

No wonder he couldn't feel close to God; it was impossible to get close to his own dad. Gary acknowledged that he was an emotional orphan. Gary had to make a conscious effort to separate his earthly father from his heavenly Father.

The first thing he needed to do was to forgive his dad for forty-five years of pain and rejection. He had never thought that this was necessary before. He believed he had overcome the past because he had become a much better father than his own father could even come close to being.

With God's help Gary walked through the steps of forgiveness and let himself admit the utter anguish that filled his soul because of the way his father treated him. He poured out the raw feelings he had been stuffing down so deep inside. He identified the hate, shame, and disgust for his father that lay dormant in his soul. Then he accepted that the answer to this kind of shame and guilt is forgiveness rather than anger or revenge. He asked God to help him forgive his father completely.

He called his dad and talked about the abuse and how it had affected his life. Gary's father was shocked to think that the things he had done could still haunt Gary today. Gary was surprised that his father was even willing to say the words "I'm sorry, son," even though he tacked on many excuses for his behavior. It didn't matter what Gary's father said; Gary knew that he could forgive his dad either way. The long overdue and much under-felt "sorry" felt good somehow. Forgiving his dad removed the obstacle that kept Gary from having the intimate relationship with God that he had always wanted. An added benefit he discovered was a deeper level of intimacy with his wife and children.

As you are moving into a deeper relationship with God through prayer, you may need to revisit parental pain (from your mom or dad or another parent figure) that is blocking you from receiving God's love. You may be realizing for the first time that you are an emotional orphan. Do you place negative character qualities from your earthly parents onto God? The way to heal from your past is through forgiveness.

Steps to Breaking Free from Earthly Parents

If you haven't come to terms with your relationship with your parents to some degree, you will be limited in how you can benefit from this book. Breaking free from earthly parents is the passageway to opening yourself more fully to God as your Father, and it happens in stages as the Holy Spirit reveals truth to you and you accept this truth and obey God's direction for healing. I see this process happening in these three stages:

1. Recognize and acknowledge the ways you place your parents' or father figure's characteristics on God. In what ways do you see God as similar to your earthly parents? How many of those ways are negative? Are you like Gary and Linda, not finding what you desire with God because you are transferring negative feelings about your earthly father onto God?
2. Open your heart to a different reality. You are doing that in some ways by picking up this book. You'll be amazed what God can do with a heart that is simply open to Him. Just tell Him that you have been seeing Him the way you saw your earthly father. Tell Him that in your own strength you are powerless to see Him differently. Ask Him to help you see Him for who He really is.
3. Forgive your earthly parents. No one has perfect parents. We are all sinners, and learning to forgive your parents is imperative. Forgiveness is a process too. It begins with a choice. Are you willing to face the fact that your parents let you down? Do you feel like an emotional orphan? Can

you forgive them for the wrongs they committed against you in the same way as Christ has forgiven you?

I believe that if you don't consciously forgive your parents, you will go through your life subconsciously trying to get the love you wanted from them through the world, your spouse, your boss, or other relationships. You will miss out on the love and relationship God wants to provide. It's the only relationship that can satisfy your soul.

The Process of Forgiveness

Through the years I have been blessed to help many people walk through the stages of forgiveness. It is like witnessing a prisoner set free or a once-wounded animal released back into the wild. By far, one of the best rewards of ministry is watching a life transformed through forgiveness. You can literally see forgiveness on the faces of people who were once burdened by bitterness as they become beacons of hope and healing. Forgiveness often comes in the three phases I will outline below.

Phase One

When I help someone through the process of forgiveness, the first step I ask them to take is to fully admit the pain and anger they have inside. This step is easy for some and almost impossible for others. People who have stuffed their anger deep inside, like Gary, have a difficult time connecting with how hurt they really are. I often suggest the person write a letter of anger that will *not* be sent to the person who has hurt him or her. The purpose is to help the person see the full extent of the wrong done to him or her. When Jesus hung on the cross to forgive our sins, He did not say, "Oh, they really aren't that bad." No, He was fully aware of the extent of our sin. Otherwise He could not have forgiven us completely. For some of us, our spirituality won't allow us to face the rage we have inside about what a parent or father figure has done to us. Don't try to forgive in your own power. Admit what is in your heart. That is the only way to open the door of your soul to God's healing touch.

Also remember that you are not perfect. You may be over-reacting or missing some information vital to understanding the things your parents said or did. That is okay. What is important is that you get out all the pain and hurt you have inside. At this point you do not need to have all the facts of why they did what they did; you just need to deal with how it felt to you. How do you feel abandoned or orphaned?

Phase Two

Next, I encourage the person trying to forgive to look at the ways they have sinned against God in response to the sin that was committed against them. You may have been a "victim" of someone else's sin, but you are totally responsible for how you respond to the sin committed against you.

In Matthew 18 Jesus told a parable to teach how ridiculous it is for us to be unwilling to forgive those who have hurt us when we have been forgiven so much by God. The parable was in response to a question that Jesus was asked. Peter wanted to know if Jesus would have His followers forgive people who had wronged them seven times. The general consensus was that a person should forgive someone three times for the same offense, but after that they were off the hook as far as forgiveness goes. Peter knew that Jesus often taught higher standards than the mainstream theology of the day, and that's why he suggested seven times. Jesus answered, "Not seven times but seventy-seven (or seven times seventy) times" (Matt. 18:22). The exact number wasn't important; Jesus meant we should forgive an unlimited number of times, and He went on to explain why by telling the parable of the unmerciful servant (Matt. 18:21–35).

A king tried to collect a million-dollar debt from a servant in his kingdom. The servant begged for forgiveness, and the king forgave the debt. That same day the servant who had been forgiven saw a fellow servant who owed him a couple hundred dollars. The servant tried to collect from the fellow servant. The fellow servant had no way to pay it back and pleaded for forgiveness. The forgiven servant refused to forgive this smaller debt and had the fellow servant and his family thrown into prison. The people were astonished and told the king what the servant had done. When the king heard this news he was angry as well, and threw the servant he had previously forgiven in prison after all. He would leave him in prison until he paid all that he owed. What did he owe? The king had already cancelled his financial debt. What he owed was the offer of forgiveness to his fellow man.

After you have expressed the anger you feel toward your parent (or others who have wronged you), the time comes for you to look at your own life. How have you allowed the pain from this person or these people to keep you from receiving all that God has for you? How have you not let God love you as Daddy? Have you been caught up in sin as a result of this sin against you? Finding the power and motivation to forgive another person is much easier when you truly receive the amazing forgiveness that God offers.

I had a difficult time convincing Gary that he should ask his father to forgive him. After all the work Gary had to do just to admit that his dad had been abusive, asking that man to forgive him seemed illogical to Gary. He took a huge step of faith when he asked his father to forgive him for harboring so much anger against him that he couldn't really let God's love into his life. Gary's admission was the opportunity for his father to say he was sorry.

You may have found relief in completing phase one by releasing the anger you feel about your parents or other authority figures. But you may not feel so comfortable looking back at yourself and facing your own sins. Doing so is important, so don't try to bypass it. You won't find the freedom you are seeking by bashing your parents. The freedom comes from acknowledging the ways they've hurt you but taking responsibility for your own life and how you have allowed your negative connection to them to keep you from connecting to God the way He made possible.

Phase Three

The last phase of forgiveness is committing to the process of forgiveness. This involves trusting God with the hurt from your life. Rather than seeking revenge or living in denial, you believe that God can do a healing work in your soul. Expect the unexpected to happen within your soul during this phase. Your part is to trust God that forgiving the wrong is the right thing to do. God will do the rest.

You need to realize that forgiveness is similar to peeling layers off an onion. You must not expect it to happen in an instant. Sometimes forgiveness can take ten minutes, and sometimes it takes ten years. What matters to God is that you have a heart that desires forgiveness. This gives Him the freedom to move deep into the recesses of your soul. He can remove the roots of bitterness that you could never reach on your own. The Holy Spirit does a work of forgiveness in your heart as you keep yourself humble before Him.

Forgiveness is like a huge weight being lifted from your soul. Where once you were a prisoner to hate, bitterness, and shame, now you are free to love the person who has harmed you the most. You see that same person through God's eyes. You want nothing more than for that person to be restored to God. In wanting their restoration, you've identified yourself more deeply with the love of God. You show your full understanding of what it means that God forgives you.

This is such an integral part to really loving God as Father. I encourage you to take it seriously. Perhaps you need to put this book down and work through this process before you read further. You might seek help from your pastor or a Christian counselor. Find a dedicated Christian with whom you can share your hurts along your journey to forgiveness.

Breaking a Positive Connection: Loving God More Than Father or Mother

What if your parents were basically good to you? Can you ever love your parents too much and miss out on knowing God as your Father?

CBS's 60 Minutes anchor Mike Wallace couldn't comprehend President George W. Bush's response to a question from Bob Woodward. In fact, Wallace's interview with Woodward was promoted with a teaser inferring that the president had something negative to say about his own father.

Actually, President George W. Bush has made the transfer of loyalty from a positive connection with his dad. He said nothing disrespectful about his father, former president George Bush, in response to Bob Woodward's question. In the 60 Minutes interview with Woodward, Mike Wallace asked, "Did Mr. Bush call his father for any advice [about the war in Iraq]?" Read the transcript of Woodward's response:

I asked the president about this. And President Bush said, "Well, no," and then he got defensive about it. Then he said something that really struck me. He said of his father, "He is the wrong father to appeal to for advice. The wrong father to go to, to appeal to in terms of strength." And then he said, "There's a higher father that I appeal to."[3]

President Bush stated that he spoke to an even more important Father about the war. In my opinion, he meant no disrespect to his highly esteemed earthly father, the forty-first president of the United States. His answer simply acknowledged that another Father is more important than a past president and even more available than an earthly father.

Luke 14:26 says, "If anyone comes to me and does not hate his father and mother, his wife and children, his brothers and sisters—yes, even his own life—he cannot be my disciple." I always thought this was such a cruel verse. Why would God suggest that we hate the people He tells us in one of the Ten Commandments to honor? At first glance it doesn't make sense. God is not instructing us to hate our parents. He is explaining that to receive everything He offers us in relationship with Him, we must be willing to transfer those deep family connections into a deeper connection to Him. I have found that we must not only forgive our father and mother but we must leave them as an important step to bonding with God as Father.

I can definitely say that separating from my parents (a piece of marriage advice God gives in Genesis 2:24) has been very important to growing deeper in my marriage, and it also has been essential to the close connection I feel with God. I have transferred my parent need to God Himself. I still love and appreciate my parents, but the Daddy bond exists only with God and me now.

I love my children so much that I want the same for them. I want them to have a closer bond with God than they have with me. I want to instill in them the fact that no matter what,

I will always be there for them, but I also want them to know that God loves them more than I could ever begin to love them. Staying too connected to your earthly parents can prevent you from knowing God as your Father.

Do you remember the feeling of watching a program or reading a book that scared you to the core? You were too old to sleep with the light on, but for some reason you just couldn't shake the fear that was haunting you. When my children had this experience, my husband and I could have allowed them to sleep in our room, or I could have gone to sleep in their room with them, but that wasn't the right solution. I talked about what I do when I get scared like that. I read Proverbs 3:24 and asked them to imagine a guardian angel sitting on their bedpost carefully watching over them. I want to teach my children how to rely on God for comfort. I know I can't be the source of comfort all their lives. I want to teach them to go to the God of all comfort.

Jesus and His Parents

The few stories we have about Jesus's family life are put there for the purpose of teaching us important spiritual lessons. A story about Jesus's preadolescence subtly displays how to make the important transfer of love and loyalty from our parents to God.

Only the Gospel of Luke gives us this insight into Jesus's life. The story was most likely told to Luke by Mary, the mother of Jesus. I think that Mary spoke about this particular event that happened when Jesus was twelve because it was the occasion when Jesus made a significant transfer of love and loyalty from His earthly parents to His heavenly Father. We get to watch it happen and recognize how to do it from Jesus's example. The story is found in Luke 2:41–52.

Every year Jesus and His parents traveled to Jerusalem for the Passover feast. The year that Jesus turned twelve, this family ritual became the occasion of a transfer of loyalty. His earthly body had matured to the verge of manhood. His spiritual life was soon to follow.

We witness this event from the perspective of Mary. Don't you know that every parent's nightmare is not knowing where their child is for days on end? Mary and Joseph had traveled for a day before they became aware that their family was in trouble. For a whole day they assumed that Jesus was with the group, just out of sight. That evening they discovered the agonizing truth—no one had seen their twelve-year-old son.

Did they sleep that night? Did they turn back to Jerusalem that very moment? What did they do about their other children?

As soon as they could, Mary and Joseph set out for Jerusalem, where they searched for Jesus over three long, heart-wrenching days. Where did they look? Perhaps they thought He was mesmerized by the big city market, so they spent a day going through all the stalls. Jesus enjoyed God's creation, so maybe they searched every quiet and lovely place they remembered Jesus taking pleasure in. They knew people who lived in Jerusalem, so maybe they went from door to door, checking with people they knew. Only on the third day did it dawn on them that perhaps they should search in the temple.

What relief flooded through them when they caught their first glimpse of Jesus sitting in the temple courts! Interrupting was rude, but after being so worried for so long, they had to express the anguish that was trapped inside.

Mary stammered, "Son, why have you treated us like this? Your father and I have been anxiously searching for you" (v. 48).

Jesus answered her, "Why were you searching for me? . . . Didn't you know that I had to be in my Father's house?" (v. 49).

Mary and Joseph didn't seem to understand his answer. The temple was the last place they thought to search.

Every parent needs to learn that they are just the earthly guardians of their children. A time comes for all children to claim their true Father. Jesus did so at twelve. He loved Mary and Joseph, but He knew He had a heavenly Father He needed to love and obey first and foremost. Although many of us can remember wanting to separate from our parents at that age, few of us knew that it was our heavenly Father we were longing to know in the way we once depended on our parents. Jesus knew.

This was the first time Jesus announced that God was His Father. He was the tender age of twelve. Are you ready to know God as Father? Are you willing to transfer your parental loyalty?

What God offers to every single one of His children is incredible to ponder. Have you ever wished that you could be a princess or a prince? Have you ever been envious of children with doting parents? I've got great news for you: you are God's child, and as God's child you *are* a prince or princess. You have a heavenly Father who loves to dote on you but always does so in a way that builds your character! We will examine this amazing truth more in the next chapter.

Reflection Questions:

1. What image of God do you see when you pray?
2. How have you been an emotional orphan?
3. How has your relationship with your earthly father affected your relationship with God?
4. How does forgiving your earthly parents open your heart to really knowing God as Father?
5. How did Jesus make a transfer of love and loyalty from His earthly parents to God?

6. Why do each of us need to transfer love and loyalty from a loving parent to God?

Intimacy Exercise:

Write a letter (that you do not intend to send) to your earthly parents about their influence, whether positive or negative, on your relationship with God.

3 You Are a Child of the King

For you did not receive a spirit that makes you a slave again to fear, but you received the Spirit of sonship. And by him we cry, "Abba, Father." The Spirit himself testifies with our spirit that we are God's children. Now if we are children, then we are heirs—heirs of God and coheirs with Christ, if indeed we share in his sufferings in order that we may also share in his glory.

Romans 8:15–17

When I speak throughout the country, I am introduced in a variety of ways, but no one has ever introduced me as who I really am. People introduce me as a Christian counselor, a women's minister, an author, a speaker. They may get personal and say that I am a wife and mother of two. They usually don't bring out that I am a maid, dog groomer, and laundry attendant. So I often reintroduce myself. I tell who I really am. Who I really am is God's daughter. And since He is the King of Kings, that makes me a princess.

It sounds too good to be true, doesn't it? The apostle John, who always spoke of himself as "the beloved," wrote in 1 John

3:1, "How great is the love the Father has lavished on us, that we should be called children of God! And that is what we are!" Who I am is a loved child of God, a princess!

Nothing has motivated my obedience, love, and devotion to God more than understanding that He sees me as His daughter and His princess.

How Do You Become Aware of Who You Are?

I believe that if each of us truly understood who we are and who God is, we would have totally changed perspectives about the problems we face. Most of our problems stem from our quest to be who we think we need to be. What is it that you like least about yourself? Is it the fact that your spouse doesn't treat you with respect? The way you yell at your children? The fact that you can't get your boss to appreciate your contributions? The way your friend is always putting you down? That you are always hiding who you really are from others? The treadmill of debt and greed you cannot get off?

The origin of all of our problems is that we do not know who we are. Genesis 1:26–28 says that we were created in the image of God. It tells us that we were created to be in relationship with God and to subdue the earth. Most of us have got it backward. We think that we are nothing and that we have to disguise our unworthiness by forcing our relationships to give us validation, acceptance, and appreciation. We try to force the creation to make us rich, beautiful, and important. We are not living in the freedom of the fact that we are created in the image of God, our relationships are meant to broaden our enjoyment of who God is, and our work (subduing the earth) is a way we can glorify our loving Creator (see also 1 Cor. 10:31).

In the eyes of your Abba-Father, you are a person of great worth, dignity, and value. God is a holy, mighty, powerful God who loves you like a daddy.

A conversation in the film version of Victor Hugo's classic novel *Les Miserables* illustrates this fact. Set in nineteenth-century France, the story demonstrates the effects of sin and the power of redemption. In one scene the hero, Jean Valjean, a former thief whose life was transformed by an encounter with a priest, becomes a factory owner and respected mayor. He discovers that his former employee, Fantine, became a prostitute after she was fired from his factory and is now near death. Jean Valjean attempts to nurture her back to health. He has a conversation with her about her illegitimate daughter, Cosette. Jean Valjean encourages Fantine to get better so she can take care of Cosette.

Fantine responds, "But you don't understand; she can't come live with me. She has no father and I am a whore."

Jean Valjean replies, "She has the Lord. He is her Father, and you are his creation. In his eyes you have never been anything but an innocent, beautiful woman."[1]

Jesus says the same about you and me: you have God, He is your Father, and in His eyes you are His deeply loved child. No matter what you have done or how you have been treated, God still claims you as His child.

Imagine God as Daddy

This isn't some pie-in-the-sky notion that I am trying to feed you to make you like yourself and even like me better. It is absolutely true! But it's not easy to digest—even King David had a hard time. He wrote,

> When I consider your heavens,
>   the work of your fingers,

the moon and the stars,
    which you have set in place,
what is man that you are mindful of him,
    the son of man that you care for him?
You made him a little lower than the heavenly beings
    and crowned him ruler with glory and honor.
You made him ruler over the works of your hands;
    you put everything under his feet.

Psalm 8:3–6

Without even knowing what Jesus did for us in making us co-heirs through His saving death on the cross, King David was mystified by God's amazing love and care for humans. As he considered the display of God's creation, he wondered how such a God could care so much for mere mortals.

Have you ever been perplexed by God's irrational love for you? Do you grasp what it means that such a magnificent and powerful God wants to have conversations with you? Can you imagine that the God of the universe wants you to call Him "Daddy"?

Philip Yancey writes, "More than any other word pictures, God chooses 'children' and 'lovers' to describe our relationship with him as being intimate and personal."[2] What do you imagine when you picture God as "Dad"?

When I imagine God as my Daddy, two qualities of a father-child relationship especially draw me to Him. One is that a daddy longs to do good to me; the other is that I can get close enough to hear a daddy whisper. A good father wants only what is best for his child. A good dad is comfortable with closeness. That kind of intimacy is reserved for special relationships. You don't experience a healthy relationship with a boss quite that way. You wouldn't really be comfortable picturing your pastor that way. Even a best friend relationship is not the same as a

51

daddy relationship. This kind of intimacy is only for a child and parent. It is different.

A childhood memory I may have in common with you is waking up terrified from a bad dream. I would jolt into consciousness so scared I couldn't move, afraid to open my eyes. The darkness that permeated my bedroom increased the intensity of my fear. But somehow I found enough courage to get out of my bed, walk from my dark bedroom down the just as dark hall, maneuver through the still dark dining room and across the unlit kitchen, arriving at the darkened door that led to my parents' bedroom. Relief flowed through my veins as I proceeded to quietly sneak into their bed and under their covers, where I found refuge from my fears. Once I got in their bed, everything was okay again.

That's the kind of relationship God longs to have with us. It's an experience of comfort, closeness, warmth, and care. Try to imagine a God who desires that kind of intimacy with you. Jesus described this longing God has to hold us close in Matthew 23:37: "O Jerusalem, Jerusalem, you who kill the prophets and stone those sent to you, how often I have longed to gather your children together, as a hen gathers her chicks under her wings, but you were not willing." These are powerful words, especially when understood in context. Jesus spoke these words just days before He would be crucified because of the accusations of the very men He was addressing. He told them how much He longed to cuddle up with them and protect them like a mother hen does her chicks. Right before expressing this remarkable longing, Jesus had blasted these same Pharisees with seven warnings, pointing out their most wanton and appalling follies. Jesus's love knows no boundaries.

Nothing about this group would have caused Jesus to love them and want to gather them under His wings. Only Jesus's character would make Him feel this way about these people. Before we start thinking we are so great because we are princes and princesses, we must remember, *His love has nothing to do with our own goodness or merit.* God loves us because God is love. It's irrational, it's undeserved, but it's true.

God loves us, and He wants to do good for us. My friend and spiritual mentor Verdell Davis Krisher quotes her first husband, Creath Davis (Focus on the Family board member killed in a plane crash in 1987): "What grieves the heart of God the most is not the bad things we do, but the good things we miss." [3] God is not half as disappointed about the bad things we do as He is about the wonderful things He can't do for us, because we won't let Him. Too often I don't live like who I really am. I don't recognize that if I come home, like the prodigal son, I will be fully received as God's child, a co-heir of Jesus Christ. God is willing to give me so much and *wants* to give me so much, but I have to be willing to receive it. Once I'm willing, the next dilemma I face is understanding what He wants to give me. How in the world could I merit the same inheritance as Jesus Christ? It doesn't seem fair; it doesn't make sense. We are exploring the irrational love of God.

Take a Look at Your Inheritance

Your mother likely warned you, "If it looks too good to be true, it probably is." When it comes to your heavenly inheritance, her advice doesn't apply. It sounds too good to be true, but it is true. I wonder if that is why God repeated the offer so many times in Scripture. If He had said it only once, would we believe it?

If you have simply accepted that you are a sinner and that you need Jesus's blood to remove your sins, you are a co-heir with Jesus Christ. Did you know that? Do you understand the value of your inheritance?

When my parents married, my father's grandmother gave them a set of dishes she had collected as free gifts that came with her laundry detergent. She didn't have a lot of money, but the glass tableware was pretty, and she thought my mother would like it. My mom had registered for fine china and received a whole table setting, so the glass dishes remained boxed up in the attic, never put on display. About twenty years later, while shopping in an antique store, she recognized her glass tableware selling for an exorbitant price. She went home and had my father pull down the box from the attic. She realized that she had more than a twelve-piece table setting of Depression-era glassware in perfect condition. She had no idea the gift was worth so much. She mainly hung onto it for the sentimental value. Not until years later did she discover its monetary worth. Most Christians are walking around with an inheritance stuck away somewhere, never exploring its value.

Many people become embittered by what they don't have. Their circumstances often cause them to doubt that God has done very much that they would consider good in their lives. Rather than examining the value of their inheritance, they feel they've been shafted by a God who has a lot to give but won't give it to them. How about you? Do you know what you have? Do you realize that you are an heir or heiress?

Webster's dictionary defines *inherit* as "receive as heir, derived from parents, succeed as heir." You do not earn an inheritance. It is a privilege granted to you by your parent. The inheritance God tells us about is also a gift. It is given from the benevolent heart of the God who has everything. He shares it with you because you are His child, not because of what you do. In Luke 12:32 Jesus tells us, "Do not be afraid, little flock, for your Father has been pleased to give you the kingdom." He gives it because it is His to give, and He has enough for every child of His to enjoy. He gives it because it gives Him pleasure.

The inheritance God gives is not worth comparing to any kind of inheritance we have ever heard of here on earth. In truth, we cannot possibly completely comprehend our full inheritance. It would be like being told you have inherited a distant planet. You've never lived there; you have heard it is wonderful and perfect, but you do not fully know your inheritance until you experience it for yourself. Here is a memo that summarizes some of what you can comprehend about your inheritance.

To: You
Date: The date of your salvation
From: God
Re: Your inheritance

As the addressee of this memo, you are hereby the recipient of an inheritance bequeathed to you by God, your Father, at the exact moment of your salvation. Being of sound mind and Spirit and under no form of duress, God the Father freely gives you what is His to give. The Father has made possible by the death of His Son Jesus Christ for you to inherit eternal life (Matt. 19:29; Col. 1:12; Heb. 9:15). When you accepted Jesus Christ as your Savior, you became wholly endowed with eternal life, even though your physical body will die. This same inheritance is equally offered to all believers. None who are without Christ as Savior will be entitled to receive this inheritance. This inheritance is a reward from your Father (Ps. 16:6; 33:12; 47:4; Col. 3:24) and is sealed by the Holy Spirit (Eph. 1:13–14).

Included in this inheritance is the land God created (Isa. 5:9; Matt. 5:5), a kingdom (1 Cor. 6:9), and the heavens which you have never visited before (Matt. 25:34; Rev. 21:1–7). The value of this inheritance cannot be measured in standard human currency. Suffice to say, your inheritance is rich (Eph. 1:18). The value of your inheritance will never decrease for all eternity (Ps. 37:18; 94:14; 1 Peter 1:4). A full explanation of this inheritance cannot be given due to the recipient's limited ability to comprehend the full impact (Heb. 11:8).

This is the gift extended to you if you are a believer in Christ. All of that is yours. And you don't have to wait until heaven to start collecting on many of the dividends. The benefits—such as praying to a God you can call Daddy, being content in all circumstances, wisdom for daily decisions, protection, and joy—are the present benefits of knowing God as Father.

Why Would Jesus Share His Inheritance?

Imagine that you grew up in a home where your father favored you above your little brother. Your dad was extra tough on him and easy on you. He always put your brother down and withheld good things from him, while he lavished favors on you. When your father died, he left a will with all the benefits of his worldly possessions going to you. Legally you owned all of your father's worldly wealth, and your little brother had been left out once again. What would you do? Would you share it equally? Would you give him a small gift from the estate? Would you justify that this is the way your father wanted it and you don't have any reason to feel guilty?

Unlike the cruel father in the example above, God loves all His children equally. Although Jesus is the only one righteous and actually deserving of His Father's love and inheritance, He is eager to fully share His riches with you. In fact, it was Jesus Himself who sealed the deal that made it possible for you to claim your inheritance.

In a study on the covenants of God found in Scripture, I had this bewildering reality brought home to me through the book of Ruth. A Jewish woman named Naomi had a husband, two sons, and an inheritance of land in Israel. Because of a famine the family left Israel and journeyed to Moab. Both of Naomi's sons married Moabite women. Naomi's husband died in Moab, then both of her sons. A destitute widow, she saw no other way to survive but to return to Israel. One of her daughters-in-law, Ruth, traveled back to Israel with her. Ruth was given special treatment in the fields of one of Naomi's relatives, Boaz. He instructed his workers to take care of her and to give her extra food.

Naomi came up with a plan for Ruth to let Boaz know that she would be interested in marriage to him. The plan worked; Boaz decided he wanted to marry Ruth. Part of the deal in marrying Ruth was purchasing the land that was Naomi's inheritance. Another relative was a closer relation than Boaz, so Boaz had to first offer him the chance to buy the land and marry Ruth. The closer relative turned Boaz down because he didn't want to risk complicating his own inheritance by marrying Ruth. Boaz was willing to take the risk.

This is an engaging story of how God was present in the suffering of an Israelite woman named Naomi and a Gentile named Ruth. It also further illustrates an aspect of Jesus's crucial decision to go to the cross. It shows that Jesus, just like Boaz, was willing to sacrifice His own inheritance for us. Jesus already has all that we are promised as our inheritance. He had it in the beginning, has it now, and always will have it. He doesn't want to keep His inheritance to Himself. He longs to share everything we could ever need or ask for, even though paying for our right to claim the inheritance meant sacrificing His own life.

Do You Live like a Prince or a Pauper?

If you really come to know God as Daddy, you will begin to live like a princess or prince. You will wake up in the home of your Daddy-King and find security in His sovereignty over the universe. You will rest assured in your inheritance, knowing that it is secure and that nothing can take it away from you. You will eagerly face each day wondering how you can enjoy time with your Father and think about the ways you can return the love He has shown you.

If we really know who we are and what is awaiting us in heaven, we wouldn't cling so desperately to the things this world offers. Most often when we pursue money, pleasure, and power, we end up missing God's gifts to us here. If we are so focused on the goal of making money, we may miss out on opportunities we have to share the gospel with others or chances to change someone's life.

Basically, responding to God's love is the key to getting the most out of life. The greatest commandment is to love God with your heart, mind, and soul (Matt. 22:36–37). If we could only picture how much He loves us, our automatic response would be absolute devotion.

Remember when the rich ruler asked Jesus, "What must I do to inherit eternal life?" (Luke 18:18). I'm not surprised that this man would have an interest in understanding more about an eternal inheritance. Like a stockbroker who has heard a rumor about a new business deal, he thought researching this question was worth his time. Jesus reminded him that he knew the commandments and listed five of them that deal with our relationship with people. The man responded that he had faithfully kept them all. (He was not only a rich man but a moral man as well.) This man did not even notice that the first four commandments, pertaining to our relationship with God, were not even mentioned by Jesus.

Because money had replaced God in this man's life, Jesus told him that he lacked only one thing. Jesus said that he could inherit eternal life if he sold everything he had and gave it to the poor.

Why did Jesus say that? This instruction revealed the true condition of the man's heart. He was happy to obey as long as he could obtain security through his money. He didn't have a heart that understood God's love for him. If he had, he wouldn't have been afraid to sell all he had; he would have known that God could replace it with more than he could imagine. And if God didn't replace the money, he would give him all he really needed here on Earth and more than he could imagine in heaven.

Do you feel favored by God? God rewards His children. He is the kind of Daddy who takes care of our most basic need—salvation—at great personal cost. He has provided for your future. Can you trust Him?

Receiving His love requires trust and brokenness. I wrote in chapter 1 that as I looked back on my spiritual experiences, I noticed a pattern emerging. One day I realized that it was this process that produced the intimacy I felt with God. I've noticed that my experiences with God happen in a cycle that beckons me deeper and deeper into a meaningful relationship with Him. The following chapters explain this process and invite you to consider how you see God drawing you into an intimate, "daddy-child" relationship.

Reflection Questions:

1. Why is it hard to believe that we are princesses/princes?
2. If our royal status has nothing to do with our merit, why should we try to do good things?
3. What are some of the good things you believe God would like to do for you if you would let Him?
4. What about your eternal inheritance motivates you to live for God here and now?
5. Have you received any benefits on Earth from your relationship with Christ? What are they?
6. Count your blessings. Write a list of benefits you receive by knowing God.

Intimacy Exercise:

Describe the ways God has blessed your life, from the simplest ways to the grandest.

Part 2

The Process of Knowing God as Daddy

4 The Basics of Brokenness

You do not delight in sacrifice, or I would bring it; you do not take pleasure in burnt offerings. The sacrifices of God are a broken spirit; a broken and contrite heart, O God, you will not despise.

Psalm 51:16–17

I remember the afternoon we sat in the doctor's office discussing my then five-year-old daughter Rachel's broken wrist. A couple weeks earlier she had fallen off a stool in a neighbor's house, which resulted in the injury. The doctor set her wrist that day and put on a bright pink cast to match her dress. Now we were back for her follow-up appointment, and the X-ray showed bad news.

"The bone is not healing straight," the doctor informed us. "Her hand will grow slightly to the right. It won't be that noticeable to others, but it could cause problems for her in the future," he warned. The only way to correct the problem was through surgery that would purposely re-break her wrist, then set it straight.

Brian and I had to make a painful decision. The discomfort of the original break was over. Inside Rachel's cast, cartilage and bone were forming to mend the wound. She was happy and playful again. We had to consent to letting her go back to the place of her pain. She had anesthesia during the break and resetting, but afterward she suffered a lot of pain and discomfort. The pain was even more intense than the original break due to the swelling from the trauma. Why would we consent to allow our daughter, whom we love, go through so much pain and brokenness *on purpose?* Because it was the only way her wrist could be made right. Right now as I type, I'm reminded that typing on a laptop could have been tedious for her if she didn't have a wrist that was correctly aligned. She may not have understood it completely at the time, but as her parents we knew that some pain in life is necessary.

You are born into this world with a sin nature. It's worse than having a crooked bone, but let's make the comparison for the sake of illustration. God knows that He could leave you alone to deal with the ill effects of your sin nature, such as death, evil, lust, greed, anger, and violence. But He loves you too much for that. The only way your sin nature can be fixed is by your being broken, admitting your sin, and receiving Jesus Christ as your Savior. You must come to Him in your brokenness in order to have your soul reset and your life made right. The apostle Paul said it this way: "If you confess with your mouth, 'Jesus is Lord' and believe in your heart that God raised him from the dead, you will be saved" (Rom. 10:9). Brokenness makes salvation possible.

The Thought of Brokenness Is Painful

We may have a little trouble believing that we are princes and princesses, but we at least find the thought pleasant. Now we turn to a quality of our relationship with Abba-Father that we often don't like. Most of us spend the majority of our lives trying to do or be something so that we can cover up the fact that we are broken. If we do focus on our brokenness at all, it is only in the context of finding a way to fix how broken we feel. Rarely do we sit and ponder that deep inside, every one of us is desperately broken. That's antithetical to our human nature.

God didn't break us, but He has the power to fix us. His power can only be released in us when we are willing to face our utter brokenness.

Brokenness Marks the Beginning of Our Relationship with God

You cannot begin a relationship with God without being broken of your wrong belief that you can do anything at all to earn acceptance from Him. You must accept your brokenness by admitting that you are a sinner. You acknowledge your own brokenness and inability when you believe that Christ's forgiveness, and nothing else, is the reason you are able to have a relationship with a holy God. At the point you are broken and admit your need for Christ, He saves you and makes it possible for you to really love God as your Father.

But that's not where brokenness ends along your spiritual journey. It takes a lot of love, work, and determination on God's part to show you who He is and why you are here. He wants to show you so much. He wants to release so much love in you. He can't get started until you come to Him with a broken spirit and a contrite heart—a heart that knows it needs healing. You need to be broken of your sin, your "God boxes," your self-reliance, your self-loathing, and everything else that stands between you and God.

God has told us over and over that the way He wants us to come to Him is with a broken and contrite heart (Ps. 51:17). He wants us to have broken hearts and not just tear our garments on the outside, as was a common practice of devout Jews (Joel 2:13). He would rather see us showing mercy than bringing a sacrifice (Hosea 6:6). God talks of the special closeness He feels with the humble (Ps. 138:6). He wants us to act justly, love mercy, and walk humbly with Him (Mic. 6:8). Jesus wants us to truly understand what it means that God, who instituted sacrifices, doesn't accept the sacrifice if the heart isn't right (Matt. 9:13).

Coming to God in a state of utter brokenness goes against our sin nature. What comes naturally is what Adam and Eve did from the moment both of their eyes were opened by their sin: they hid. We have been hiding ever since. We hide as an attempt to cover up our brokenness.

My favorite way to hide has been through self-sufficiency. The rest of the world may not have been able to see it, but I regularly set goals for myself and put forth the effort to attain them. From my grade point average in school to putting myself through graduate school to even the weight I would maintain, I was self-sufficient.

That was working great for me (I thought) until I got married, had children, and needed to keep a house, work part time, and volunteer in my church and community. I became a mess! All the self-sufficiency in the world couldn't keep up with my responsibilities.

When I finally admitted how powerless I was, I learned how powerful God could be through me. God had to do a lot of work in me to break me of self-sufficiency, and sometimes I have a tendency to run back to the mirage that I can do it by myself. But I love the freedom I have found by coming out of hiding. When I am broken and admit, "I can't," God is quick to hear my cry and become my strength. "I am powerless" has been the most powerful prayer I've ever learned to pray! I waited years before I let God lure me out of hiding and invite me to lean on Him instead.

How Do You Hide from Brokenness?

First Adam and Eve hid from each other. They grabbed fig leaves and sewed them together to make coverings for their naked bodies (Gen. 3:7). They didn't want to be seen unclothed in front of each other after sin entered the world. Next they hid in the bushes from God when they heard Him walking in the garden and calling their names (Gen. 3:8–9).

We have become a human race of natural-born hiders. We are quite refined in the craft of hiding. Many even find the church a safe place to hide from facing brokenness before God, rationalizing, "If I attend every activity and give my money, time, and talents to the church, I don't have to face what a sinner I really am." Hiding at church may help you avoid facing your sin, but it doesn't do anything to change it.

We can hide from or avoid brokenness in many ways. Perfectionism is a natural favorite. It is the opposite of what God desires. It is the mind-set of setting unrealistic goals (that seem attainable to the perfectionist) for yourself and others. The perfectionist never achieves her goals, but she hides by believing that one day she will and trying ever harder.

Another common way to hide (and my personal favorite) rather than being broken is the path of self-sufficiency. Like for the perfectionist, it is all up to you, but unlike the perfectionist you do have room for error. The Pharisees were self-sufficient religious people who never considered the way of brokenness. Why would they need to be broken and contrite when they could work it all out by making and following their own rules for pleasing God?

Others choose the path of anger to hide their brokenness. Anger is a strong emotion, and it feels much more powerful than the vulnerability of brokenness. The anger can be focused at self, God, or others. But it always serves the same purpose: to help you hide from facing what is really wrong.

Addictions are rampant. You can use quite a number of pleasure-seeking ways to numb yourself from the pain you feel about your broken state. Addictions can be to drugs, alcohol, sex, shopping, work, gambling, sports, exercise, food, TV, movies, video games—the list goes on and on. Some of our addictions are applauded by the world, while others bring shame and disgust. Either way, they function by keeping you numb to your broken condition.

Materialism is another favorite of many in Western society. Why do we want to get so much? What do we think we will have when we get it all? Will having it all help us erase the brokenness we feel? No, but we never know for sure, because we never get enough.

One way of hiding that may surprise you is spirituality. This includes reading the Bible to get a formula to make yourself feel good about who you are or what you do. You may control your anger, forgive everyone, give your money to the church—all good things. But if the focus is on you feeling superior, not on a relationship with God, you may be hiding behind these good actions.

What Is Your Way of Hiding?

I mentioned what an expert I had become in using self-sufficiency to cover my brokenness. How have you covered yours? Take this short quiz to see if it helps you confirm your style of hiding.

Answer the questions yes or no, then count up your yes answers for each section.

Perfectionism

1. I usually have to do tasks myself because others do not do things "right."
2. I would never leave the house wearing wrinkled clothes.
3. If it is not done right, it should be thrown out.
4. My closest friends and family consider me a perfectionist.
5. God only loves me when I do things perfectly.

Number of yes answers: _____

Self-Sufficiency

1. God expects me to figure out what He wants and do it.
2. A lot of people count on me to keep things going.
3. "Where there's a will, there's a way" is my motto.
4. I love the feeling I get when I do it myself.
5. God doesn't want to be bothered about our lives.

Number of yes answers: _____

Anger

1. If people only did the right thing, I wouldn't get so angry.
2. I can't control the fact that I get angry.
3. People complain about my angry reactions.
4. I put someone down at least once a day.

5. I don't understand where the anger inside me comes from.

Number of yes answers: _____

Addictions

1. I can say I am compulsive about one thing (i.e., food, shopping, alcohol).
2. I have tried to quit more than once and failed.
3. I have made a New Year's resolution to quit a behavior and failed.
4. I don't feel I have control over a certain behavior.
5. My behavior gives me a feeling of relief.

Number of yes answers: _____

Materialism

1. I spend more money than I make.
2. I constantly compare what I have to what others have.
3. I can't wait to show or tell people about my latest purchase.
4. I feel good about myself when I have more material possessions than other people.
5. I don't let my debt keep me from purchasing more.

Number of yes answers: _____

Spirituality

1. I can say I do mostly what God wants me to.
2. I never get angry, because the Bible tells me not to.

3. People call me a "spiritual giant" or "pillar of the church."
4. People expect great things out of me.
5. I am at church every time the doors are open.

Number of yes answers: _____

Look at the total number of "yes" answers in each category. Which category is the highest for you? You can use several ways of hiding, so don't be surprised if you have more than one category that has a high score. You could also hide in a style I haven't mentioned here. Only when you come out of hiding and are courageous enough to admit you are broken will you begin to taste intimacy with God. You have so much to gain through brokenness.

The Positive Side of Brokenness

Jesus said we need to be like children if we are going to inherit the kingdom of God (Luke 18:16–17). You cannot know God as Daddy unless you are willing to acknowledge that you are His child. My teenage children do not like the terms *mommy* and *daddy*. Those names don't bother them behind the closed doors of our home, but they can be mortifying in public. Nonetheless, I still prefer to think of myself as their mommy and my husband as their daddy, although I refrain from using those names in front of others.

The terms *mommy* and *daddy* express a uniquely dependent relationship. Ironically, deeper intimacy with God requires immaturity. A blessed regression takes place in our relationship with God. Spiritual maturity means becoming more childlike.

What appears to be immaturity—still calling on your Daddy—is actually spiritual greatness. Max Lucado wrote:

At our house we have had a banner year. Our third daughter has learned how to swim. That means that all three can walk. Three can swim. And two out of three have the training wheels off their bikes. With each achievement they have delightedly pointed out, "Look, Dad, I can do it on my own." Deanalyn and I have applauded and celebrated each accomplishment our daughters have made. Their maturity and mobility is good and necessary, but I hope they never get to the point where they are too grown up to call their daddy. God feels the same way about us.[1]

By now Max Lucado's girls are well past training wheels, but I'm sure he still feels the same. All parents long to see their child grow up and achieve milestones yet still yearn to keep that unique closeness and bond that is characteristic of younger childhood.

Some of my most cherished memories of motherhood are of times when my children delighted in me. I was their hero. They loved being with me. They wanted me the most. They knew I was bigger, someone they could trust, and someone they needed. What happened to those little ones? They grew up to be teenagers. They doubt everything I say and would rather spend time with their friends than me! I know it's a natural part of their development, but I miss those days when I was thought of so highly.

God delights when we have childlike wonder in our relationship with Him. Rather than focusing on ourselves, what we are missing, or what is not going well in our lives, we live in awe of Him and what a wonderful Daddy-God He is. This is the way a young child admires his parent. That kind of relationship is satisfying to God and also to you, His child.

Think about it. Remember how simple life is for a child who has a good daddy? She never worries about what she will eat, how to pay the electric bill, whether her daddy loves her or not. She is secure. She is established. She is safe! Her life centers around her daddy. He is the one who makes decisions that are always for her good. She is happy to trust in his safe embrace.

This is the way Jesus lived His life on earth. He related to His Father as a child (Luke 2:49). He didn't worry about what He would eat (Mark 8:17), how to pay bills (Matt. 17:24–27), or whether He was loved (Mark 9:7). His life centered on His Daddy (John 5:19). God gave Him instructions and He always followed them, though He was free to disobey. Everything God told Jesus always worked for the best in Jesus's life. He was happy to trust in God's safe embrace (Mark 14:36).

Jesus Embraced Brokenness

Jesus was broken for us when He was willing to come to this earth as a little child. He was broken when He did only what His Father told Him to do and not what others told Him. Of course, the ultimate way Jesus was broken was by going to the cross because of our sins. With every act of brokenness Jesus demonstrated, He reaped God's blessing beyond measure. At the name of Jesus every knee will bow (Phil. 2:10–11).

If you let it, brokenness will have that same effect in your life. It will lead you to the place that you most want to be—in intimate relationship with God. Let's look at some common ways that we need to be broken in order to allow God's love to deeply penetrate our souls.

1. Broken from Mom and Dad

We have already looked in chapter 2 at the importance of transferring your love and loyalty from your parents to God. Breaking from your earthly parents is necessary to make space in your heart for God as your Father.

One of the ways we hide is by clinging to our parents to get them to love us and to prove that we are lovable. Some of us miss out on the extraordinary love of God as Daddy because we are too satisfied with our parents' love or so fixated on finally getting them to approve of us and love us that it drains our energy.

Jesus showed us the importance of breaking away from earthly parents and family in a healthy way. He didn't break away from His parents because they were abusive. He did it because it was part of His spiritual journey. In Luke 8:19–21, when He was told that His mother and siblings couldn't get past the crowd to join Him, He didn't get up right away and push some people out in order to make room for them to come in. Instead He said, "My mother and brothers are those who hear God's word and put it into practice" (v. 21).

Some never break away from their parents because they never got the love they needed. Psalm 27:10 says, "Though my father and mother forsake me, the LORD will receive me." The King James Version uses a more descriptive rendering of what exactly God does for us: "When my father and my mother forsake me, the LORD will take me up." It is a picture of the Father picking up His child and holding him in His arms.

Dealing with the pain of feeling forsaken by my human parents was my bridge to knowing my heavenly Father as Daddy. My parents love me dearly, but they can't help but "forsake" me in some ways. Honestly, I'm grateful for the fact that my parents have failed to love me perfectly, because it has been the avenue through which I've come to know and experience God's love most deeply.

I remember several times as an adult that I felt hurt by my parents' decisions or by statements they made to me. On one of these occasions, I cried out to God in my depression and despair from the pain of what I was feeling. God reminded me of Jesus's words from the cross: "My God, my God, why have you forsaken me?" (Mark 15:34). Instantly, I received comfort from the reality that Jesus knew the pain I was feeling. He comforted me in my brokenness and showed me that breaking away from earthly parents is part of the process of bonding more fully with Him.

I pray that any unintentional pain that I've caused in my children's lives will be for them a pathway to knowing God, who will never, under any circumstances, forsake them. As much as I love my children, I know there have been and will be times when they feel forsaken by me. The truth is, they will never be forsaken by God. Maybe you have been intentionally hurt by your parents. Do you trust that as a Christian you can never be forsaken by God?

2. Broken of Self-Reliance

One of the greatest obstacles to experiencing an intimate relationship with Jesus Christ is self-reliance. God delights in assigning us seemingly impossible tasks so that we can discover that replacing self-reliance with God-reliance is the energy of the Christian life.

I can't count the number of times I have failed in ministry because I tried to do it in my own strength. God-reliance has been a hard lesson for me to learn. God-reliance begins when you have the attitude of Christ. Everything Jesus did was for the purpose of bringing glory to His Father. You have God-reliance when you are not living your life to get the spotlight to shine on you. Rather, you want all the light on Christ.

You shine the light on God through humility and dependence. Micah 6:8 tells us what God wants most for us is that we act justly, love mercy, and walk humbly with God. Jesus demonstrated all these qualities, especially humility. Even though Jesus existed in the form of God, He did not consider equality with God something to be grasped, but He humbled Himself

(Phil. 2:5–11). Jesus totally relied on God's plans and purposes for His life.

Adam and Eve were created in the image of God, but they *did* consider equality with God something to be grasped—and look what happened to them and to the rest of us as a result of their decision. You can see how we have been following in their footsteps. God wants to show us how much better our lives can be when we totally rely on Him.

3. Broken of Your Own Perspective

Jesus's humility was also revealed by His absolute dependence on the wisdom of God. Isaiah 55:8–9 says, "'For my thoughts are not your thoughts, neither are your ways my ways,' declares the Lord. 'As the heavens are higher than the earth, so are my ways higher than your ways and my thoughts than your thoughts.'" Do you believe that God's ways are better than your ways?

I meet people every day who are stressed and bombarded by pain. Some can see their part in creating their pain through choosing to disobey God's Word. Others are in pain due to the sinful choices of others or because of circumstances they had no power to prevent. They have a moment or long periods of feeling like Jeremiah in Lamentations 3:17–18: "I have been deprived of peace; I have forgotten what prosperity is. So I say, 'My splendor is gone and all that I had hoped from the Lord.'" Have your life circumstances ever brought you to a place of absolute despair like Jeremiah?

When we stop defining God based on our limited perspective, on our circumstances, or how we are being treated by others, we are making spiritual progress. We live in a sin-filled world. This reality alone does much to pervert our knowledge of God. Faith requires childlike trust, believing what God tells you about Himself in His Word no matter what is happening in your life.

Jeremiah didn't crawl into a corner and die when his life experiences left him totally impoverished. Jeremiah's childlike faith was what delivered him from despair. Just after he expresses his inner anguish, he writes, "Yet this I call to mind and therefore I have hope: Because of the LORD's great love we are not consumed, for his compassions never fail. They are new every morning; great is your faithfulness. I say to myself, 'The LORD is my portion; therefore I will wait for him'" (Lam. 3:21–24).

If you are to have the right perspective on your earthly experiences, you must understand that this world is not the place God wants you to live eternally. A child may not understand why she has to wait while her brother is already tall enough to ride a certain ride at the amusement park. She must trust her caregiver that the waiting is for her good and serves a purpose. The child's cognitive development prohibits her from fully comprehending the whole situation. Every way she reasons, the rule appears to be unfair and unkind. But if the child trusts her caregiver, then she believes it will all work out for the best in the end, even if she can't comprehend it from her own perspective.

Are you willing to be broken of clinging to your own perspective and willing to release your future completely to God? When growing closer to God, you must be willing to think outside the box. You must be satisfied that you will never fully comprehend God. Like Jeremiah, you need to learn to delight in what you know to be true of God.

4. Broken of "God-Boxes"

Many times our own self-created image of God blocks us from loving God. That's why God spoke so strongly in the second commandment against creating an idol to worship (Exod. 20:4–6). Many of us have created an image of God as a cruel party-pooper, a rigid and rule-keeping Being who spends His whole existence trying to catch us having fun so He can ruin it. If you are going to learn to pray as Jesus did, perhaps the first step you need to take is to be broken of your own notion of God. Louis Evely said, "Everyone has his own preconceived notion of God which nothing can change; but that, too, we must give up—that, before all else."[2]

For me, coming to know God as Daddy has meant turning away from many of my former beliefs about God. My journey has caused me to ponder the wonder of God rather than put Him in boxes that make me feel comfortable and think that I can control Him.

The stronger your God-box, the less aware you are that you have one. I remember the first time I realized that God was not a "Fundamental Baptist" (the denomination I grew up in). It hit me while I was reading books from a variety of denominations, periods in history, and theological backgrounds. These books did more to draw me into a deeper and more personal relationship with God than my Baptist teaching alone. It suddenly dawned on me—God is not a Fundamental Baptist, nor is He a Catholic. He loves both, but He is defined by neither.

Perhaps just reading this book is releasing God from the box you put Him in. Maybe you have never considered that God would want you to call Him "Daddy."

5. Broken of Self-Loathing

Jesus made it clear that He did not come into the world to condemn the world. The world was condemned already. God sent His Son Jesus to "uncondemn" us (John 3:17–18). Relationship with Jesus does not define who is condemned; it defines who is saved. If you are going to honestly move forward in your relationship with Daddy-God, you must stop accepting Satan's condemnation of you. Your own self-loathing can be what is

78

keeping you from seeing yourself for who you really are: God's child, a prince or princess. Romans 8:1 says, "Therefore, there is now no condemnation for those who are in Christ Jesus." God's Word says there is *none*, no condemnation! How often do you condemn yourself? Can you set aside your own standard for yourself and accept yourself the way God sees you? Your commitment to your own self-loathing will distance you from intimacy with God.

Brokenness Leads to Comfort

Once you are broken of your earthly parents, your self-reliance, your own perspective, your God-boxes, and your self-loathing, you will receive what your soul most longs for: comfort. The comfort of Abba-Father, Daddy-God is worth any brokenness you experience. His comfort makes the brokenness worthwhile. God's comfort heals you and brings some degree of enlightenment to your brokenness. In the context of God's comfort, brokenness can even begin to make sense. Let's discover how.

Reflection Questions:

1. How is brokenness related to salvation?
2. In what ways was Jesus broken?
3. Why is brokenness necessary?
4. How have you been broken of your parents? Of your self-reliance? Of your own perspective? Of your God-boxes?
5. How does self-loathing hinder your intimacy with God? How can you be broken of this self-loathing?

Intimacy Exercise:

List the most broken moments of your life. Beside each, write what you learned about God because of your heartache.

5 The Healing Power of Comfort

The LORD is close to the brokenhearted and saves those who are crushed in spirit.

Psalm 34:18

Think of a time in your life when you felt closest to God. Was it during a crisis, hardship, or difficulty, or was it during a time when everything was pretty good in your life? Many people would answer that they sensed God's presence most intensely when they were most desperate. I remember the first time I felt God's presence with me; it was at a point of absolute heartache.

I was eighteen years old and far away from home. My heart had been torn in two by a broken relationship—a situation I thank God for now but which totally devastated me at the time. I awoke during the night in turmoil from the despair that flooded my heart, feeling like I had no one to turn to. I began to pray through my tears when suddenly, as I turned over, I felt God's presence in a way that I had never experienced before. I felt as if God were holding me. His embrace was warm but different from any human touch I had ever known. I felt as if I were encircled by a cloud. No part of me was untouched by His comfort. I had never had a feeling like that before, and although I enjoyed it, the comfort of His presence caused me to drift slowly to sleep. The next morning I read Psalm 34:18: "The LORD is close to the brokenhearted and saves those who are crushed in spirit."

I had no idea of the magnitude that experience would have on my life. I awoke to exactly the same circumstances and emotional heartbreak that caused such anguish of soul the night before. My situation had not changed at all, but I had been dramatically altered. I was different! Receiving God's comfort transformed my life.

Every day I meet people who have not only weathered tragic circumstances but also suffer emotional and mental difficulties that are the result of either sins committed against them or sins they have committed. One of the ways I lead them to healing is through teaching them to receive God's comfort. Everyone who has received God's comfort is deeply changed by the experience.

Over the years I've met many who say they have never known God as intimately as when they encountered Him through suffering. As they share their experience of God's comfort during their suffering, they concur about an unbelievable development in their view of suffering. Although they would never ask for pain, they would not trade the hardship for the experience of drawing closer to God.

My husband calls our friend Lois Ward "Miracle Woman." After a high-speed, five-car accident she lay in a hospital bed with a broken back. During her recovery a large blood clot traveled straight to her lungs, causing a massive blockage and heart failure. She went into a coma and was placed on a breathing machine for three days. Her condition was presumed fatal. But by God's grace, Lois is walking around today with little residual pain from her tragic ordeal.

She told me about a conversation she had with her daughter Emily. Emily asked, "If there was any part of your life you would change, what would it be?" Lois locked eyes with her, thinking Emily would probably wonder if her response would be her car accident. Instead, Lois answered emphatically, "Not my accident." She would never want to give up that part of her life, because it was one of the times that she was most aware of God's comfort and presence in her life.

If you have ever experienced God's comfort, you understand why someone would even go so far as to choose the greatest pain she suffered in her life if not experiencing it would mean never knowing God's comfort. In 2 Corinthians 1:3 God is called "the God of all comfort." Knowing God as comfort is one of the highlights of our spiritual lives.

A World in Need of Comfort

Each of us suffers. The only difference is the degree to which some suffer. I have never suffered hunger because food was unavailable to me. Yet many people all over the globe wake each morning not knowing if they will find food to fill their stomachs. God has sent me on mission trips to meet these people. It has enriched my life dramatically.

God doesn't send me to their countries to bring them all back to America and give them the same opportunities I have to get food. I can't directly change the governments or economic systems in the countries where they live. God sends me anyway. He tells me I can give them something: I can encourage their faith. I can help them know what can never be taken from them (Luke 10:42). I can pray for them. I can bring some physical relief through financial gifts.

What I have discovered in the lives of these desperately poor Christians is that many of them have a spiritual wealth that far exceeds my own. They may not know how they are going to eat today, but they have faith and spiritual maturity that humbles and astonishes me.

God's ultimate plan to comfort us is found in the words of John 3:16: "For God so loved the world that he gave his one and only Son, that whoever believes in him shall not perish but have eternal life." God's desire to comfort us is revealed in Revelation 21:1–5, where He tells us how He will make all things new. Included in His description of heaven is the fact that "He will wipe every tear from their eyes. There will be no more death or mourning or crying or pain, for the old order of things has passed away" (v. 4).

Some Christians cannot see that God is good because they see their own or others' suffering. God has a purpose for allowing sin that causes suffering. He did not demolish the whole world back when Adam and Eve sinned. God gave Adam and Eve a second chance to choose to trust Him, and He does the same for you and me. The fact that this world keeps on spinning in spite of its corrupt nature is evidence of God's passion to bring us back into relationship with Him. First Corinthians 15:21–22 says, "For since death came through a man, the resurrection of the dead comes also through a man. For as in Adam all die, so in Christ all will be made alive." God didn't destroy the world after Adam and Eve sinned because He didn't want to destroy any humans who would choose Him over the Deceiver. God tolerates suffering on Earth in order to deliver us from eternal suffering. According to God's Word, He has the power to make all things—even the suffering in your life—work together for good for those who love Him and are called according to His purpose (Rom. 8:28).

God is acutely aware of our need for comfort. Mrs. Charles E. Cowman wrote in her best-selling devotional *Streams in the Desert*, "Nearly all God's jewels are crystallized tears."[1] God never ignores His children's cries. He may have reasons we do not understand for allowing our pain. But He is not ignorant, distant, or indifferent to our pain. It affects Him deeply. Psalm 103:13 says that God is a Father full of compassion. Brokenness is God's passageway to the most tender places of our souls. This is the place in you that is in greatest need of a Father full of compassion.

Brokenness Opens Your Heart to God's Comfort

Henri Nouwen calls receiving God's comfort "going into the place of your pain" in his book *The Inner Voice of Love*. In fact, that book was originally a personal journal Nouwen kept during a six-month period of dark depression in his life. In the midst of a crisis and desperate to try anything just to feel better, he felt God telling him to face his pain instead.

We don't like to feel our pain. We take aspirin so we won't feel a headache. We do anything we can to manage pain. But God invites us, with His tender help, to face our pain.

Henri Nouwen describes our desire to avoid the place of our pain: "You are so afraid of that place that you think of it as a place of death. Your instinct for survival makes you run away and go looking for something else that can give you a sense of at-homeness, even though you know full well that it can't be found out in the world."[2]

Most people miss God's comfort because they find ways to numb themselves from their pain instead. For some the numbing agent may be drugs, alcohol, food, work, excessive shopping, or other addictive behaviors. Others numb themselves in less obvious ways, like people pleasing, exercise, and distractions. None of these, however, offers the closeness and fulfillment that only the God of all comfort can give.

What keeps us on our quest to remedy our pain with everything but God is a simple lack of awareness that God is bigger than our pain. Perhaps you don't trust God because you feel He failed to protect you from whatever agonizing experience you've had to endure. Perhaps you don't believe He could bring anything good out of circumstances like yours. Maybe you're even thinking, *If He were really a better God, maybe I wouldn't be dealing with this pain in the first place.*

The only way you can begin to move through your pain and into God's comfort is to realize that God is, without question, bigger than your pain. Henri Nouwen puts it this way: "You have to begin to trust that your experience of emptiness is not the final experience, that beyond it is a place where you are being held in love."[3] Pain management is not your only option; God can genuinely heal through receiving His comfort.

In Psalm 73:21–28, the psalmist poignantly describes the process we go through to receive God's comfort. Our pain often causes us to turn against God in anger (vv. 21–22). Anger against God makes us ignorant. When we accuse God we behave like a brute beast—an irrational creature instinctively operating out of fear and pain. While we flail around in grief and bitterness, God never leaves us; in fact, He holds our right hand (v. 23). His presence is our comfort. Once we let God into our pain, we will see Him in a whole new light (vv. 24–28). We come back to our senses when we consider important questions like "Whom have I in heaven but you?" (v. 25). We remember who God is. He becomes our strength, portion, and refuge (vv. 26–28).

Receiving God's comfort is the only true healing of your pain. Face the place of your pain with the belief that God is there and that His arms of love can hold you and sustain you. You must, as Nouwen reminds us, "weep over your lost pains so that they can gradually leave you and you can become free to live fully in the new place without melancholy of homesickness."[4]

You cannot be comforted by God without knowing Him as your Daddy-God. I discovered the wonder of calling Him "Daddy" as I saw that He is good in the midst of my pain.

I already told you about the heartbroken encounter with God I had as a teenager. I had not been taught the Scriptures about "Abba" Father at that time, but the memory of that encounter with God helped me receive that message when it was taught to me later in my life. My heart accepted that it must be true that God would want me to call Him "Daddy." He had comforted me like a concerned Father that night in my total despair.

Since then I've had more pain to deal with. Each experience of God's comfort has solidified my belief that God really is as wonderful as He says He is. That's why I can be so confident in writing this book. I know that God is greater than my pain. I'm positive that He is greater than yours!

The Experience of Comfort

I often compare the experience I have when God comforts me to the way I comforted my babies when they developed ear infections in the middle of the night. Due to immature ear canals, frequent infections in the ears are an inevitable experience of childhood. Both of my children had at least a dozen of these, and I learned to recognize the symptoms. When one of them woke in the middle of the night crying with fever, I was pretty sure what was causing the problem. The only thing was, no doctor was willing to meet me at 3:00 a.m. to diagnose my child's ear infection and prescribe antibiotics to cure it. I had to do what most mothers do. I waited until 8:30 a.m. and started calling until I finally got through to make the earliest appointment available.

In the meantime, I offered comfort that made a difference in my child's life. My comfort didn't cure her problem. The healing wouldn't begin until morning. Still, my comfort was a powerful force to soothe her pain. I would pick her up, give her pain medication, and hold her close. Without comfort she was totally alone in her agony; now she had me near. Holding her upright made the intensity of the painful fluid in her ear ease a bit. Giving her pain medication helped lower her fever. But the main thing I did was be with her in her pain, letting her know I cared. It was enough. It made a significant impact on her pain.

This is the way I have experienced God's comfort. Many times, He doesn't fix or change the painful situation that is causing my grief. Rather, He holds me close in the midst of it. I know He is there. I am no longer isolated and alone. I trust that He knows and understands what I am going through. I have to trust that He may have reasons beyond my understanding for not making the suffering go away. I believe that God's love is bigger than my pain, and I feel safe in spite of my sadness.

Ironically, if the painful circumstance instantly disappeared, I wouldn't have the opportunity to experience the power of God's comfort. If I had no problems to contend with, then I wouldn't become convinced that God is bigger than my problems. I wouldn't know the intimacy of allowing myself to be held in the arms of my Father, my Daddy-God and my true safety.

Jesus Was in Need of Comfort

Hebrews 12:2 says: "Let us fix our eyes on Jesus, the author and perfecter of our faith, who for the joy set before him endured the cross, scorning its shame, and sat down at the right hand of the throne of God." This Scripture speaks volumes to me about Jesus's own need for and experience of comfort. Jesus was destined to walk through a valley of death and shame we cannot fully fathom. The cross has become a symbol of love, peace, and healing to us today. We often lose touch with the reality of what the cross meant for Jesus. The shame of the cross was a violent contrast to the existence Jesus had always known. The cross was utter and complete degradation, an experience which brought Him to the outer limits of agony. Think of it as beyond any suffering you or I could ever experience.

On the night Jesus was subjected to the greatest degree of suffering any human has ever experienced, He received God's comfort. Luke's account of Jesus's garden prayer reveals the depth of the spiritual, emotional, and physical suffering Jesus faced. Luke 22:44 says, "And being in anguish, he prayed more earnestly, and his sweat was like drops of blood falling to the ground." Without a doubt Jesus was facing the most extreme symptoms of human stress. His bloody sweat evidenced the severity of the anguish in His soul.

We see the results of God's comforting Jesus that night in the garden. Before and during the prayer Jesus's heart was in anguish. After the prayer and being ministered to by angels, He got up, ready to face the fact that the cross was the only way. Hebrews 12:2 helps me understand how God comforted Jesus. Jesus was comforted from the thought of the joy that would come after His suffering. The thought of being reconciled with God and making it possible for redeemed humans to be with God and have eternal life enabled Jesus to endure the shame of the cross. The future joy made the present anguish bearable. God comforts us with the same joy. This life is definitely not all there is. God has so much more for us. The thought of joy in heaven comforts the soul.

The Bond of Comfort

The bond formed between you and God, during the poignant moments of your life, confirms His love for you. Psalm

23:4 has become one of my favorite verses. I have lived its truth, and it has forever changed the relationship I have with God to know that "even though I walk through the valley of the shadow of death, I will fear no evil, for you are with me; your rod and your staff, they comfort me." God's presence is comfort.

Presently, I serve as the women's minister at my church in Texas. In my position, I had the privilege of helping launch a ministry to women whose lives have been touched by cancer. God raised up three leaders to get this group started. I met with each of them individually, then we all met together. Though they had different experiences with cancer, they had one thing in common. Each of them would say that their journey through cancer brought them closer to God than they had ever been before.

On the other hand, sometimes I listen to people grumble and complain about how awful God is as they recite the litany of their sufferings. They look to their circumstances to define God rather than looking to God to define their circumstances. First Thessalonians 5:16–18 says, "Rejoice always; pray without ceasing; in everything give thanks; for this is God's will for you in Christ Jesus" (NASB). When you follow these directions, you find a peace that others may not be able to understand. That's not to say that when you look at God you will fully comprehend why a horrendous thing is happening to you. You can, however, comprehend that it is not happening to you without God's knowledge or without His presence, grace, and strength to endure it. The difference between a cursing Christian and a comforted one is that the former is seeing God as indifferent to their suffering and the other is seeing God as close, concerned, and caring. The only way you can possibly give thanks in all circumstances is by seeing God for who He really is.

Seeing God for Who He Really Is

God is not the creator of suffering or sin; Satan is. When you accuse God of not loving you because your life has pain, you reveal your ignorance of God. God created everything good in this world. God never forsakes you, even when you are angry with Him. Not seeing God for who He really is caused Satan's downfall. God created Satan with amazing glory, but Satan wanted more. Satan was not happy with who God really is, and he thought he could become better than God. He thought he could re-create a world without God. He was totally wrong, but that hasn't kept him from trying to convince us that God is the source of our suffering and that He is far away from us.

When you read the psalms of David you will find a pattern. First, David bemoans his unjust circumstances; then he remembers God's character and goodness. When David looks at his circumstances, he is in anguish; when he sees God for who He really is, he is at peace. What changes is his awareness of God's attributes and God's presence in his life. Awareness of God's character overcomes suffering and gives birth to comfort.

The Purpose of Suffering and Brokenness

Beyond allowing us to experience the comfort of God, our suffering also produces character in us. James 1:2–4 explains: "Consider it all joy, my brethren, when you encounter various trials, knowing that the testing of your faith produces endurance. And let endurance have its perfect result, that you may be perfect and complete, lacking in nothing" (NASB). Peter is even so bold as to say, "Therefore, since Christ has suffered in the flesh, arm yourselves also with the same purpose, because he who has suffered in the flesh has ceased from sin" (1 Peter

4:1 NASB). Are you aware of a painful experience in your life that has birthed character in you?

The character we develop makes us journeymates for others needing to meet God in their suffering. Oswald Chambers says, "The way to find our self is in the fires of sorrow. . . . If you receive yourself in the fires of sorrow, God will make you nourishment for other people."[5] And 2 Corinthians 1:3–5 says, "Blessed be the God and Father of our Lord Jesus Christ, the Father of mercies and God of all comfort, who comforts us in all our affliction so that we will be able to comfort those who are in any affliction with the comfort with which we ourselves are comforted by God. For just as the sufferings of Christ are ours in abundance, so also our comfort is abundant through Christ" (NASB).

Not only do we serve a God whose genuine comfort is larger than our suffering, we also live with humans who are in desperate need of comfort. As you experience the comfort of God in your suffering, you will grow in character and will be able to share the reality of God's comfort with others.

God's comfort mends your heart. Suffering either opens your soul to receiving God's comfort or traps you in a litany of self-pity. Second Corinthians 1:3–6 tells us that God comforts us in our troubles *so that* we will be able to comfort others also. When we receive God's comfort ourselves, comfort will naturally flow out of our lives to others. That is exactly what is happening in the cancer support group that we started in our church's women's ministry. Those ladies wouldn't have anything to give to others if they hadn't been comforted by the God of all comfort (2 Cor. 1:3). Paul told the Philippians that if they had received comfort from Jesus's love, then it was time to move into action as a witness for Christ (see Philippians 2).

An open soul clings to God's Word for comfort. Your Daddy-child relationship begins through brokenness. It is cemented through the comfort you experience when His presence and

His Word penetrate your pain. Next we will look at how God's Word fuels our intimate relationship.

Reflection Questions:

1. In what ways do you seek comfort when you are in pain?
2. Do you tend to blame God for your pain or cry out to Him for comfort?
3. What is God's ultimate comfort?
4. How did Jesus receive God's comfort?
5. How are we bonded to God through comfort?
6. How does the way we experience suffering reveal how we really see God?

Intimacy Exercise:

Write about the most painful reality in your life right now. Invite God to comfort you. How can you see God as bigger than your pain? How is He present in your pain?

6 Responding to the Light

The secret things belong to the LORD our God, but the things revealed belong to us and to our children forever, that we may follow all the words of this law.

Deuteronomy 29:29

Karen slammed her Bible closed. Then, as if catching herself in an act of disrespect, she gently laid it on the coffee table but turned away from its view. She had been sitting on her couch, praying and pleading with God to tell her what to do about her life. The spiritual exercise that had been given to her by her associate pastor left her angry and afraid. The Scripture she had just read stood in stark contrast to what she thought was best. Karen had been a Christian for ten years but had stopped attending church and reading her Bible lately. Tim, her current boyfriend, was the main reason. He was also the reason she was so upset with what the Bible had to say.

One year ago Karen was living her same old "good girl" life. She seemed happy but not totally fulfilled. Then Tim walked in. He came into her office to sell advertising, and from the moment he shook her hand, she felt mesmerized by his persona. Keeping a professional demeanor, she quickly fell back on her business savvy to make the deal. Some of her admiration for Tim must have been evident over the course of their meeting, though, because that very afternoon he called her back and asked her to meet him for a drink. Karen had never gone out for drinks after work, and she didn't know how the answer "yes" blurted out of her mouth. The rest of the afternoon at work she was useless; she couldn't keep her mind on anything but Tim. All she and her secretary seemed able to talk about was the fact that Tim was the kind of guy the phrase "tall, dark, and handsome" was meant to define.

The relationship pretty much took off from there. Before long Karen was doing a lot of things that in the past she'd always taken pride in being too "Christian" to do, like calling in sick when she wasn't, dropping out of church, and blowing off her closest friends. She got fired from her job for lying and poor work habits. She even started having sex with her boyfriend, and before long moved in with him.

Tim was her life. He made her feel good. So what if she couldn't be completely sure that he was faithful? Did it really matter that he was paying their bills with her credit card? After all, his sales job was going to make them both rich; all she needed to do was hang in there. Things were going to change any day.

Or so she thought, anyway. But after the last fight ended with Tim shoving her into the wall and running out of the apartment with the $200 in cash she had just withdrawn from her account, Karen started to wonder if life with Tim was everything she had built it up to be.

That's when she stopped by her old church. She could get in right away to talk to the associate pastor, and he listened as her story flooded out through tears and shame. Gently, he told her to ask God if she should break off the relationship with Tim.

He suggested she write a prayer to God asking Him to guide her with His Word to know what she should do. He asked her to then read Scripture and record what God said.

Karen didn't have time to talk to God that night because Tim came home with a sweet card, a heartfelt apology, and promises that he would never hurt her again. Even so, the next day, she wrote her prayer.

"God," she wrote, "could you make Tim stop fooling around with other girls and save our relationship?" The pastor had asked her to simply start reading the Bible where she had left off long ago. Since she hadn't opened her Bible in over a year, she looked for her bookmark and began reading in 2 Corinthians 6. By the time she got to verse 14, she knew that God was giving her His answer. This verse seemed to be speaking straight to her: "Do not be yoked together with unbelievers. For what do righteousness and wickedness have in common? Or what fellowship can light have with darkness?"

Karen knew this passage well and had often thought about it when she was first falling in love with Tim. Now God hadn't answered her prayer the way she wanted. In fact, He had told her the very opposite of what she wanted to hear: "Break up with Tim." The decision Karen would now make in response to reading God's Word depended on who she believed loved her more—Tim or God.

Do You Believe That Father Knows Best?

True obedience comes down to answering this question: "Do I really believe that God loves me and wouldn't ask me to do anything that would hurt me?" God does give us rules and guidance for how to live our lives. Everything He tells us to do is for our own good (see Deut. 6:24).

All of God's rules help you live well and long on the earth. Moses pleaded with the Israelites to obey God's Word. He wrote, "And now, O Israel, what does the LORD your God ask of you but to fear the LORD your God, to walk in all his ways, to love him, to serve the LORD your God with all your heart and with all your soul, and to observe the LORD's commands and decrees that I am giving you today for your own good?" (Deut. 10:12–13). Moses considered it a privilege, not a hardship, to have God's Word to follow. He wrote, "The secret things belong to the LORD our God, but the things revealed belong to us and to our children forever, that we may follow all the words of this law" (Deut. 29:29).

Most of the time we think obeying God means giving up something we really want for something that makes God happy and us miserable. That is simply wrong. When we obey God it does make Him happy, but obeying God is always for our good!

The parable of the prodigal son (Luke 15:11–31) brings out this reality. Jesus told the story to show us our relationship with the Father. He wanted to remind us that though we, like the prodigal son, abandon God in our determination to live life our own way, we are invited home to a welcoming Father who wants to wrap His arms around us and hold us in a loving embrace.

In this same story we are introduced to the older son who never left home; rather he tirelessly worked for the father and kept all the rules. Jesus shows us that the older son's refusal to go in to the party was just as insulting to the father as asking for money, leaving home, and squandering the gift. The older son thinks that his relationship with his father is based on his obedience and all the work he does for the father. Jesus's story showed us God's point of view.

God doesn't want us to serve and obey Him out of duty. God wants obedience motivated by love and trust. In his final message to the Israelites, Moses pleaded with them to obey God out of trust in His love and goodness to them. We clearly see God's heart when He says, "Oh, that their hearts would be inclined to fear me and keep all my commands always, so that it might go well with them and their children forever!" (Deut. 5:29). God also is the one who causes us to want to obey Him (Phil. 2:12–13). He says in Ezekiel, "And I will put my Spirit in you and move you to follow my decrees and be careful to keep my laws" (Ezek. 36:27).

Just as a loving father wouldn't send an unprepared child into the world without instruction, so our loving heavenly Father uses His Word to teach us how to live life with the best outcome. Since giving the nation of Israel the Ten Commandments, God has continued sharing with those He loves His guidance on living. It's not just advice. Obedience to His Word is necessary for a meaningful relationship with Him. Jesus made it clear that a close, intimate relationship with God involves obedience, explaining, "If you love me, you will obey what I command" (John 14:15). Psalm 107:43 says, "Whoever is wise, let him heed these things and consider the great love of the LORD." You cannot truly obey God without loving Him.

Karen is at a turning point in her life. She can keep trying to make her relationship with Tim replace her relationship with God, or she can take a chance and see how restoring a relationship with God will affect her relationship with Tim. God has told her to break up with Tim. Does Karen trust that God is good and would never ask her to do something that would harm her? This is the big question in life. Do you trust God enough to let Him guide and direct your life?

Jeremiah 29:11–14 tells us,

> "For I know the plans I have for you," declares the LORD, "plans to prosper you and not to harm you, plans to give you hope and a future. Then you will call upon me and come and pray to me,

and I will listen to you. You will seek me and find me when you seek me with all your heart. I will be found by you," declares the LORD, "and will bring you back from captivity. I will gather you from all the nations and places where I have banished you," declares the LORD, "and will bring you back to the place from which I carried you into exile."

God doesn't play hide and seek with us. He wants to show us good things. But He gives one condition: you have to seek Him to find Him. He's not hiding. If you are sincere about a relationship with Him, you will open your heart to Him. You will seek Him with all your heart. The main ways that we seek God with our hearts are through reading His Word, doing His will, prayer, and walking in His Spirit.

The Father Gives His Word to Guide Your Life

The most compelling evidence that God wants to have an intimate relationship with us is His Word. He wrote it from His heart and even guaranteed that no promise of His will be broken (Titus 1:2). I am absolutely amazed to realize how God has preserved His Word for us and also how personally it can be applied to our lives. Here is an example, told by Robert Morgan:

Dick and Margaret Hillis were missionaries in China during the Japanese invasion. Dick developed appendicitis and would have died unless he was taken by ricksha to the hospital. On January 15, 1941, with deep foreboding, his wife Margaret watched him leave.

Soon the local Chinese colonel came with news: the Japanese army was near and the townspeople must evacuate. Margaret knew her one-year-old son and two-year-old daughter would never survive as refugees, so she stayed in her home. Early the next morning she tore the page from the wall calendar and read the new day's Bible verse. It was Psalm 56:3—"What time I am afraid, I will trust in thee." The town emptied, leaving Margaret and her children alone and feeling abandoned. The next morning she read the verse for the day, from Psalm 9:10—"Thou Lord, hast not forsaken them that seek thee." The next morning she rose to distant sounds of gunfire and worried about food for her children. The calendar verse for the day was Genesis 50:21, "I will nourish you and your little ones." An elderly woman suddenly stopped with a pail of goat's milk, and another person brought a basket of eggs.

Through the day and night, sounds of warfare increased and Margaret prayed for deliverance. The next morning she read on her calendar Psalm 56:9—"When I cry unto Thee, then shall my enemies turn back." Invasion seemed imminent.

But the next morning, all was quiet. Villagers began returning to their homes. The colonel knocked on her door. For some reason, he told her, the Japanese had withdrawn. No one knew why, but the danger was gone and they were safe. Margaret glanced at her wall calendar and knew she had been reading the handwriting of God.[1]

Margaret's story magnifies just how personal and pertinent God's Word is. Though Margaret heard the enemy approach her village, the handwriting on the wall (the calendar with Scripture references chosen many months prior by someone who would have no way of knowing Margaret's predicament) told a different story. God had planned these things from long ago (Isa. 25:1).

My own experience has been similar. Many times what I read in God's Word goes against my wisdom regarding a situation. For instance, on one occasion I started my time with God angry at my husband and wanting God to really let him have it, or at least for God to join me in a little righteous indignation. I didn't expect God to tell *me* to do better. Right there where I was reading that day, in the middle of Revelation of all places, God spoke to me about how I needed to change. God said, "Stop being like the accuser of the brethren; look at your own sins instead." I know it's not easy when God's Word seems impossible to follow. His Word is full of divine absurdities.

How you respond to God's Word is a litmus test detecting how much you *really* love God. Jesus challenged our true love for Him by stating, "If you love me, you will obey what I command" (John 14:15). Is His Word a lamp to your feet and light for your path (Ps. 119:105)?

The Father Reveals His Will and Invites You to Follow

Most people want to know what God's will for their lives is so that they can consider it as an option and contrast it to what they have in mind. Karen is in a position like that. She wants God's will to be that her boyfriend Tim will change. She wants to get closer to God, but she doesn't want to lose Tim. Fully committing ourselves to God involves accepting that our lives are bigger than we can understand. To grow more intimate with God, you must trust His love for you more than what you think is best. Following God's will involves mystery. His plan does not always make sense to us.

One of God's mysteries that touched my life was the birth and death of my nephew Daniel. Daniel was my sister and brother-in-law's first child. He was born with Down syndrome and other birth defects. He spent approximately half of his short life in the hospital. Daniel died at the age of two and a half from complications after surgery to correct a birth defect. In fact, in his short life he underwent numerous surgeries and suffered tremendous pain with each procedure. Each time he approached death, his petite body would rally and give us hope of a full recovery. But on May 28, 1988, Daniel left this life of struggling behind to enter the peace of heaven. I have sometimes wondered, *Why didn't he make it, with all of our prayers and hopes? Why did Daniel have to suffer so much for the brief time he lived on this earth? Why did my sister and brother-in-law have to face such sorrow and pain only to lose their son in the end?*

Though I do not have answers to these questions, I do have comforting thoughts. I think about how much Daniel meant to me, even though I saw him only three times. I know that he made a huge impression on his doctors and nurses and the pastor who visited him frequently. My brother-in-law and sister believe he was an angel given to us for just a short time.

All these thoughts help reveal the meaning of Daniel's life, but they don't answer all of my questions. No answers on this side of heaven will be enough. The biggest question is, "Can I still believe that God is good, even though He allowed so much suffering in Daniel's life?"

God may ask us to do things that don't seem reasonable. For instance, you may be overcommitted financially and in debt. God's Word tells you to give the first 10 percent of the money you earn to him. You might reason, "That is stupid; I should use that money to get out of debt." Actually, in the process you develop financial discipline as you earmark 10 percent of your income for God. It causes you to become more thoughtful with the 90 percent you have left. If you follow God's plan, it will help you get out of debt. Some things God asks us to do don't make sense rationally, but they do spiritually. You can discern the secret of His wisdom only as you do God's will.

When I was in college, my spiritual life was deeply impacted by reading a biography of George Muller. What impressed me most about his life was not the number of orphanages he started in England but the manner in which he decided to begin each new ministry. He would have an idea for a ministry, then go into his prayer closet and pray until he didn't care whether God said yes or no to the idea—he just wanted God's will.

I've used this example in seeking God's will about all the major decisions of my life since then. A recent decision to become a women's minister was made with this approach. I knew since 1994 that God had called me to work on a church staff. I assumed that God would call me to work on the same staff as my husband. I waited patiently for the opportunity. It never came. When I found out about a position at another church in town, I sensed in my spirit that I would be disobeying God if I did not send my resume. I did, but I was sure God would shut it down. He didn't. Instead He changed my heart through the process and showed me it could work for my husband and me to be at two different churches. God expects us to follow His will even when it doesn't make sense.

The Father Desires Honest Relationship

I am responsible for bathing our dog Aggie once a week. You should see his face when he realizes it is bath time. He is such a pathetic sight. But the minute I set him free after his bath, his personality totally changes. He is happy and excited. He runs all over the house in absolute bliss.

God always has to nag me into confession, and sometimes I pretend that I am confessing when I'm really just practicing a spiritual duty. I've got to ask myself why. What's so difficult about taking a shower for my soul? Why do I want to stay in my sin and dirtiness when I can be clean?

Like I do with my dog Aggie, God drags me kicking and screaming into His cleansing presence. The most amazing thing happens when I confess my sin: I am instantly sparkling clean. I stand in Christ's righteousness. I know that is why Satan works so hard to draw me away from confessing prayers. He knows that the breastplate of righteousness is my greatest defense against his attacks on my life (see Ephesians 6).

Prayers that get noticed in heaven are the kind that speak the truth of what is actually happening, not what we think God wants to hear. A daddy delights in the humble honesty of his son or daughter, not in their cunning ways of disguising the truth.

You can pray eloquent prayers or vivacious ones, and precious are the prayers of a little child. Yet according to Jesus the best kind of praying is the gut-purging kind that goes like this: "God, have mercy on me, a sinner" (Luke 18:13–14). We really get close to God when we are totally honest about ourselves in prayer.

Did you ever break a prized possession of your parents' and find yourself stunned by their sane and rational response to your complete honesty? Honesty never disappoints the heart of a daddy. Honest prayer will get the attention of God.

Prayer Can Feel as Intimate as Cuddling Up on God's Lap

Most of us pray like we write a Christmas wish list: "Give me, give me, give me . . ." Others pray memorized words with little thought behind them: "We thank thee, Lord, for these and our many blessings. Amen." When you get right down to it, prayer is opening your heart to the heart of God. It is communication between a humble human being and the God who created the universe. An intimate relationship with God is cultivated through prayer. When you pray, you place yourself in the presence of God. When your prayers are sincere, they open your mind to God's wisdom. Through prayer God can turn your anxiety to peace (Phil. 4:6). He can turn your neediness into satisfaction (Matt. 6:33). He will turn your burdens into rest (Matt. 11:28–30).

R. C. Trench says, "We must not conceive of prayer as an overcoming of God's reluctance, but as a laying hold of His highest willingness."[2] This is one of the hardest realities for us to grasp.

In fact, it was the downfall of Adam and Eve. Doubting God's goodness is the reason we miss out on intimacy with God.

Prayer is cuddling up on God's lap. I know that sounds a little sacrilegious, but it's true. I loved it when my children sat on my lap. I remember holding them in my lap when they were little and sensing I was getting a little taste of heaven as I held them close. I didn't care what my children had accomplished or even how they smelled. I just loved holding them. It felt good for them to be there and good that they wanted to be there.

God wants to hold us close. The problem is that most of us won't let ourselves be held by Him. You have to be willing to come just as you are, smelly and unaccomplished, to be held by God. I have a stubborn flaw of not wanting to see myself as I really am. I would rather focus on the things I like about myself. I am an author, a counselor, a Bible teacher. I do good things, I give money to the church, and sometimes I don't yell at my husband. I live as if in a house full of distorted mirrors. They entice me to feel good about myself and distort who I really am. When I let myself be held by God, I realize that God loves me even as I really am.

Do you pray "Abba, Father"? Next time you pray, envision God as your loving Father inviting you to come and sit on His lap. He doesn't mind that you smell. Let Him show you who you can be. Believe that His ways are good and learn to do what He tells you to do. Trust that you can tell Him anything, and He will help you find the path of truth.

The Father Gives His Spirit to Help You Obey His Word

The Holy Spirit was the greatest remedy for living in a sin-filled world that God could give. God knows what is going on down here. He knows you are tempted to follow paths different from His plans. He knows that painful emotions are hard to face and that because of that many become addicted to drugs, alcohol, sex, shopping, work, and more. He knows that loving your enemies seems impossible for hurting and angry victims. He knows that finding meaning and purpose each day is not easy.

He sent the Holy Spirit to enable you to live the way He shows you. The Holy Spirit was so important that the early Christians were instructed not to leave Jerusalem until the Holy Spirit came to them (Acts 1:4–5). Today, you receive the Holy Spirit when you admit your sin and accept that Jesus's death allows you to be God's child. God comes to live in you. Only through the Holy Spirit can you and I even begin to obey and please God. The Holy Spirit gives us wisdom to follow God's plans. The more you are filled with the Holy Spirit, the better you will become at recognizing God's presence.

Through the Holy Spirit we learn how to call God "Daddy" (Rom. 8:15). The Holy Spirit reminds me of things I need to do. He gives me ideas and wisdom for the books and articles I write. He tells me when I am sinning. He gives me insight into other people's needs. I recognize that the Spirit of God living inside me helps me connect to people as I share God's truths. His Spirit gives me passion as I pray. God living in me through His Spirit opens my heart to trust that God loves me more than an earthly daddy ever could. When Jesus was teaching the disciples to pray, He described the Holy Spirit as the greatest gift God could give us. In Luke 11:11–13 He says, "Which of you fathers, if your son asks for a fish, will give him a snake instead? Or if he asks for an egg, will give him a scorpion? If you then, though you are evil, know how to give good gifts to your children, how much more will your Father in heaven give the Holy Sprit to those who ask him!" When you ask God for a relationship, He doesn't give a picture of Himself. He actually gives you a *part* of Himself. He gives you the Holy Spirit. He does this because He is your good Father.

All of this is evident in my life by the way I obey Him. There is no getting around it: intimacy with God is fostered through obedience. When I obey God, I change. I'm no longer a weak, sin-filled, selfish mess. I have strength, wisdom, and power that is not my own. Titus 2:14 explains this change: "[Christ] gave himself for us to redeem us from all wickedness and to purify for himself a people that are his very own, eager to do what is good." When the Spirit helps you obey, you begin to actually take on the strength and power of your Daddy, the next point of the cycle.

Reflection Questions:

1. How does God as Father know best?
2. How is obedience to God as Father linked to intimacy with Him?
3. When has God given you direct instructions in His Word?
4. How does God show you His will for specific decisions in your life?
5. How does the Holy Spirit help you know how to obey?
6. Why is it a privilege and not a sacrifice to be given His law to follow (Deut. 29:29)?

Intimacy Exercise:

List the things you are doing because God has told you to do them. List the things God has told you to do that you are not doing. What benefits have you received from obeying God's Word? How does that motivate you to obey Him about the issues on your second list? Step out in obedience about one of those issues this week.

7 The Power of Relationship

Because you are sons, God sent the Spirit of his Son into our hearts, the Spirit who calls out, "Abba, Father."

Galatians 4:6

There were five of them. All males, all of the same race, all determined to stir up trouble and cause damage. Not that the five teenage boys couldn't find enough to do on a Friday night. They were only yards away from a football stadium that had been filled with football fans from their school and another. The game, the cheerleaders, the crowd, and the food from the concession stand were not enough excitement for them. No, they wanted to feel the power of taking someone down. This night would not be complete for them unless they got a chance to prove how tough they were. They wanted to look into the eyes of a victim; they wanted to feel the power of jumping a helpless target.

Not too far from the stadium, on the path to the parking lot, they staked out their prey. It had to be someone walking alone. That way they were sure to carry out their heinous deed and not risk a foul-up by jumping a guy who had a friend. Five on one are good odds. The victim couldn't be too big either; after all, what would it do to their egos if the victim fought back and took a swing at them? They needed the right person. A big man walked by—he *was* alone, but he looked *too* big. They weren't certain he couldn't hurt them back. Here came a group of four . . . too many. Just at the right time, between the groups of passersby, a thirteen-year-old boy came walking through the parking lot. Alone. Seeing their chance, all five jumped him. They didn't choose him because of something he did. They had never seen him before. They didn't choose him because he looked at them. He never even saw them; they tackled him from behind. They did it because they could. They did it because he was a different race, he was smaller than they were, and he was alone.

What they didn't realize was that the big guy who had previously walked by—the one that might put up a fight—was this boy's father. And although he had already made it to the car, he was keeping an eagle eye out for his son, waiting for him to arrive so they could go home together. Imagine what that father did the minute he saw his son in trouble. He made a beeline for those boys, arousing the attention and assistance of everyone else in the parking lot.

You should have seen those "tough boys" run when they saw how this father responded. The scramble to get out of there was fast and furious, but not fast enough—the dad was able to memorize the license plate on their car. The police were called and the bruises assessed. How differently the night would have ended if that boy's father hadn't been there! The thirteen-year-old boy didn't have a chance fighting off a gang of five older kids, but a protective father had all the strength that was needed. That's how our heavenly Father helps us in our weakness (Ps. 91:14–16).

The young boy learned that night that when your Daddy is watching out for you, you have a power greater than your own. A relationship with God produces a supernatural transformation from your limited power and resources to His *unlimited* power. A mighty force is unleashed within you when you discover the intimacy of a Daddy-child relationship with God.

When Has God Been a Powerful Force in Your Life?

Perhaps God has been a powerful force for you but you haven't given Him credit. I can't wait to find out when I get to heaven about the ways He overcame evil on my behalf. I know that I have been spared many potentially fatal car accidents. Many days on my driving journeys I have been certain an angel was involved in the prevention of harm coming to me on the road. This is not because God loves me more than others whose accidents weren't prevented. It is simply because *that* particular accident at *that* particular time was not God's plan for me, and God's plans cannot be thwarted (Job 42:2).

I love reading *Guideposts* and *Angels of Earth* magazines. They share numerous stories of how God has been a powerful force in someone's life. One example is "A Flash of White" by Dana Christmas. She was a resident assistant during her senior year of college when a fire broke out in the dorm. She used every ounce of her strength attempting to wake sleeping students to get them out of the fire. When her strength was gone, she says, "I glimpsed a flash of white. Then strong arms embraced me, lifting me, raising me up. As we moved slowly through the blackness I no longer felt pain. I couldn't see him, but the man held me tight. I heard a door slam, and I felt us descending a stairway, escaping into the night."

After she awoke in the hospital, she learned that she had saved many lives that night. When a friend recalled seeing her walk alone out of the dorm, the doctor confirmed what she knew:

she could not possibly have walked down the stairs and out of the building with the severity of her injuries. God had been her strength when her own was gone.[1]

Relying on God Is Hard to Do

Even though I know that God is the power force for my life, I usually end up trying to do things in my own strength first. Do you know how hard it is to write a book, run a household, work part time, and be involved in my church and community? I must confess that I still have moments when I feel totally overwhelmed by my to-do list. But over the last ten years or so, I have definitely changed. If you could pull down my prayer journals from ten years ago, you would find the musings of an overwhelmed woman. I had two young children then, and I thought they took a lot of time and effort during the preschool years. I didn't realize that as they grew older they would have to be driven many places and have homework, church responsibilities, and schedules of their own. All this makes life just as intense as when they were in the toddler years, if not more so! The pressures of family life have increased. The difference is that I've changed.

I've learned how to rely on the guidance of God in the things I choose to do. I make sure I am not wasting time on things that God hasn't called me to do. Then I do the things He does ask of me in *His* strength. Consequently, I'm now doing more than ever, but only because I'm doing it in God's strength. I don't feel overwhelmed. Three qualities of my life emerge when I am relying on God:

1. My burden is light.

Jesus promised that His burden is light. Matthew 11:28–30 says, "Come to me, all you who are weary and burdened, and I will give you rest. Take my yoke upon you and learn from me, for I am gentle and humble in heart, and you will find rest for your souls. For my yoke is easy and my burden is light." Most of the overburdened people I meet are weighed down because they are wearing the yokes that belong to other people. They wear their wife's yoke, their best friend's yoke, their children's yoke, their husband's yoke, their boss's yoke, and their mother's yoke. Taking off the overburdening yokes that belong to other people is the first step in unburdening your life and finding the strength you need. Jesus promises us that if we are yoked with Him, our burden will be light. The only way we can experience a light burden is by tapping into a strength that is not our own.

Yokes were made of wood and used by farmers to help keep the oxen in place as they plowed a field. A yoke that fit properly enabled the oxen to plow together in harmony, sharing the load. Jesus doesn't describe the Christian life as a collar with a leash but as a yoke. God doesn't become yoked with you to control you. He yokes with you because you were not created to bear burdens on your own. You are meant to be yoked to Jesus. When you are yoked to Christ, your burden will feel light.

2. I'm not a power seeker.

When Jesus offers us His strength, He is by no means saying, "Come to me and I will give you power to do all the things you want to do but don't have the energy, strength, or expertise to do on your own." We all would like more strength than we have. We readily pay money, spend time, and exert effort on exercises, eating plans, vitamins, or anything else that seems to offer more strength. Jesus was not making the kind of offer proposed on a Saturday morning infomercial. His offer of strength and not feeling overwhelmed by your life involves being yoked with Him. It involves doing His work, the things that God created you to do. You will be given the strength to do whatever God has laid out for you to do.

Even when I am doing what God has called me to do, I must consider what I am really after. When I write a book or speak at a conference, I want to know if I have made a difference. I want to feel good about myself. I want you to like my book. I want you to tell your friend how it changed your life. I want to feel powerful and good.

Serving God to feel powerful in my life or to get the approval of other people doesn't cut it. That's not why God gives us power. Humility is essential for the power of God to be released in us. Luke 3:21 says, "When all the people were being baptized, Jesus was baptized too." Pictures of Jesus's baptism by John the Baptist are so common and beautiful that we rarely question the spiritual irony it depicts. Here we find Jesus being baptized right alongside the sinners of the world. Why should He be baptized when He was without sin? Even John the Baptist objected to the absurdity of it. But the Father spoke well of Jesus's utter humility. The Spirit revealed Himself in bodily form as a dove.

We must be eager to walk into the waters of baptism through our repentance, for when we do, we instantly hear God the Father's words of approval and explanation of our identity: "You are my Son [daughter], whom I love; with you I am well pleased" (Luke 3:22). At once the power of the Holy Spirit is released in us.

When I put aside my ego needs and walk in humility, I re-member what a privilege I have to share His message. I stop focusing on the book sales I will make and instead find myself focused on what God wants me to say. It is similar to the way Paul described his preaching in 1 Corinthians 2:4: "My message and my preaching were not with wise and persuasive words, but with a demonstration of the Spirit's power." This power that is greater than your own is not some kind of superpower that is given so you can have more control. This power requires reliance on a strength you cannot see but you know is there. Oswald Chambers advised, "Rely on the certainty of God's redemptive power, and He will create His own life in souls."[2]

Power-hungry people that we are, we want to grasp the power of God and use it to execute our own plans. God knows better than to give in to our power-hungry plans. He does this to protect us, because we wouldn't have the slightest idea how to use His power if He relinquished it without constraint. We would abuse it. The only way the power of God can do good through us is if we stay yoked with Christ.

3. I give up on my own plans.

When I ask for God's power to do something I want to do for Him, God often gives me an idea I never would have thought of on my own. Ephesians 3:20 says God is "able to do immeasurably more than all we ask or imagine, according to his power that is at work within us." I am simply amazed that God would even be willing to work within us, but the truth is that He does, and His work is beyond our wildest imaginations.

In the book of Judges, we are introduced to Gideon, who is from the smallest tribe of Israel and from a clan considered weak even in his unimportant part of town. No one would expect a guy like Gideon to lead a nation to victory in war. For seven years the Midianites were oppressing the Israelites. How could a guy like Gideon do anything about it?

Judges 6 has the answer: "The LORD answered, 'I will be with you, and you will strike down all the Midianites together'" (v. 16). God promises His power and His resources, but He doesn't want me to deceive myself into thinking that the power getting it done is mine. No, it gets done because of *God's* power working *in* me. After God convinced Gideon that He was going to use him to lead the army of the nation of Israel to victory, Gideon was a changed man. The most unlikely general of Israel's army subsequently unified thirty-two-thousand men willing to go to battle. Anybody could see God had been at work in that situation.

That wasn't good enough, according to God's plan. If Gideon led those thirty-two-thousand Israelites against the Midianites, they might believe that they defeated their enemy in their own strength. This would be spiritually devastating for Israel, because in such a case, they wouldn't even think about God. They'd go on living their lives for themselves, disregarding God once again. The peace they achieved probably wouldn't last five years. No, God had to be sure that Israel knew that it was God's power that defeated the Midianites.

So God had Gideon weed down the army. First, Gideon told them that anyone who was the least bit scared should exit right now. Twenty-two thousand men took him up on the offer, leaving a measly ten thousand men to fight. That was still too many, so God had Gideon choose only three hundred to actually go up and fight against the Midianites. God doesn't give strength so we can boast. He explained to Gideon, "You have too many men for me to deliver Midian into their hands. . . . Israel may not boast against me that her own strength has saved her" (Judg. 7:2). God's power is a wonderful power. But it is God's power. Don't forget that. Don't think you've got God's power all bottled up in a jar that you can use at your own discretion. God is too wise to give us His power in that way.

This is also why Jesus instructed the early church to wait in Jerusalem until the Holy Spirit came upon them. They needed the Spirit of God to become God's witnesses (Acts 1:8). Not only would they fall flat on their faces if they tried to do it in their own strength, but they also would get a sense it was up to them. Each of us is "God's workmanship, created in Christ Jesus to do good works, which God prepared in advance for us to do" (Eph. 2:10). In doing God's work the power of God is released in us. As the power is released in us, we enjoy a unity with God that fills our hearts and our lives.

Jeremiah 9:23–24 reminds us, "This is what the LORD says: 'Let not the wise man boast of his wisdom or the strong man boast of his strength or the rich man boast of his riches, but let him who boasts boast about this: that he understands and knows me, that I am the LORD, who exercises kindness, justice and righteousness on earth, for in these I delight.'" Jesus told the seventy-two witnesses not to rejoice that the evil spirits obeyed them, but that their names were written in the Book of Life (Luke 10:20).

Don't overlook the powerful force God has been in your life, like the Israelites did. Deuteronomy 1:29–33 summarizes their journey: "Then I said to you, 'Do not be terrified; do not be afraid of them. The LORD your God, who is going before you, will fight for you, as he did for you in Egypt, before your very eyes, and in the desert. There you saw how the LORD your God carried you, as a father carries his son, all the way you went until you reached this place.'"

When You Feel Your Strength Is Gone

Even though I am well acquainted with the wonder of God's power, I still find myself in a quandary about my powerlessness. My own spiritual journey amazes me. Knowing what I know, why do I attempt to do some things in my own power over and over again? I always end up falling flat on my face.

When I find myself failing in that way, I ask myself these three questions:

1. Is my burden too heavy because I'm not doing what God called me to do?

This world offers many more good things to do than I will ever have time and resources to do. Powerlessness in my life is often a sign that I've taken charge of my life again and am doing things, even good things, that God hasn't called me to do. In order to be ready to do what God has called me to do, I need permission to say no to the requests that are not from Him.

God designed a rhythm of work and rest in the universe. We Westerners try to ignore our need for rest. We think we can bypass God's design. You can be sure that if you are constantly feeling overwhelmed by what you need to do, you may be doing things you have no business doing.

I am amazed that Jesus had the power to heal every single human being on Earth of any disease, even death, but God's purpose for Him wasn't to raise everyone who had died or heal every disease. Jesus focused on God's purpose. He only healed the people God showed Him to heal. He only raised certain people from the dead. We must accept God's limits.

2. Am I trying to get attention for myself?

We all want to be loved! I've been shocked by how many times I have been tempted to claim God's power as my own. I ask God to bless the ministry He has given me to do. He does. People thank me and praise me. I accept their praise—and fail to give God credit.

Every one of us was born with a deep longing for love. Sometimes this desire for love can lead us to do things that look like serving God but are really trying to get love and attention for ourselves. This is not the kind of service that God empowers—not because He is a selfish God but because He wants the absolute best for us. The love we are searching for cannot be found through human approval. Yes, it mimics God's love, but it's not the real thing. He is a God full of love and approval who takes deep pleasure in you, but He won't enable you to deceive yourself. Even though I personally have stumbled more times than I care to remember, seeking my own approval, I am grateful He let me fall. Sometimes failure is the only way God can get my attention back on Him where it needs to be.

I remember my early years as a Christian speaker. I wanted everyone to be impressed with what a great speaker I was. But the evaluations of my talks began to come back with criticism. The director of the program couldn't understand why people were so harsh in their comments. She felt my presentations were equal to others that received positive feedback. I'm not sure if my talks were as bad as my evaluations said they were, but I can tell you for sure that God used that experience to challenge my goal of speaking of Him to draw attention to myself.

3. Am I making my own plans and asking God to bless them?

Listening to God and waiting on Him for direction in my life isn't easy. I can be very hard on myself. I often set unrealistic goals that I can't possibly reach. Sometimes when I put them down on paper, God shows me that I'm not following Him. Rather, I'm focused on getting the approval of others.

I am a big-time planner. Early in our marriage this used to threaten my husband, Brian. He felt he had to come through on all the dreams I would suggest for our future. Now he just smiles and dreams with me. I tend to think God agrees with all my plans for my life. When He doesn't make something that I counted on happen, I am disappointed at first. Later, I'm glad that He won't let me totally plan my life. I thank Him that His plans cannot be thwarted in my life (Job 42:2).

When I am doing what Jesus wants me to do, I feel the way Paul described the Christian life in 2 Corinthians 2:14: "Thanks be to God, who always leads us in triumphal procession in Christ and through us spreads everywhere the fragrance of the knowledge of him." What Paul says is absolutely true—God gives me the strength to do His work. And when I don't have the strength, it's not because God failed. Often it's because I stopped relying on Him. If I'm not feeling triumphant, something is wrong with the intimate connection between us.

Spiritual Energy

Are you aware of a spiritual energy that flows through you when you are doing what God calls you to do? If you are intimately connected to God, you will feel it. It is evidence of your deepening intimacy with God. Although I have experienced this intimacy many times, I still get disconnected from God from time to time. Just when I think I am facing impossible odds, answered prayer (sometimes from prayers I forgot to pray) saves the day.

Sometimes I have a radio interview, a retreat to lead, and a field trip at my child's school to attend, all within forty-eight hours. I look at that schedule and admit, "God, I am powerless to manage these three things plus all the laundry, packing, and other details in between." After that prayer, I simply begin to do what I can do, and amazingly, it all gets done in a strength that is not my own. Not only that, but I feel God's strength in little ways too. He doesn't just give me power to accomplish the spiritual things I do; He works through me to do the everyday things as well. Is it any surprise that "I am powerless" is the most powerful prayer you can pray?

God is my tower of strength. When has God been a tower of strength for you? God the Father was Jesus's tower of strength every day, giving Him the strength, wisdom, and power to do everything He was sent to Earth to do. Those same resources are offered to you. If you don't have them now or have never experienced God's strength, get prepared. A sign of deep intimacy with God is a recognition of His power released in your life. Out of you will flow streams of living water (John 4:14). At this point, when you literally feel God's power working through you, you begin to sense how much you are loved. You discover the depth of intimacy God offers.

Reflection Questions:

1. How does a daddy provide strength for his child?
2. How have you sensed God giving you power in your life?
3. Why is it so hard to rely on God?
4. How does Jesus make burdens light?
5. Why doesn't God just give His power to us to use as we want?
6. How does surrendering your plans relate to receiving God's power?

Intimacy Exercise:

Record the ways God has been your strength this past week. If you aren't aware of Him as your strength, look for the ways you can see Him as your strength in the coming week.

8 The Depth of Intimacy

Be imitators of God, therefore, as dearly loved children.

Ephesians 5:1

Everyone on my block envied Lucy. Her mom made her the center of the universe. Every night she meticulously curled Lucy's hair into banana curls. What second grader in the early seventies wouldn't admire a perfectly coiled banana curl? Lucy's store-bought plaid skirts and knee socks were coveted by every second grader in our class. Lucy's house was the closest to our school, yet her mom walked halfway there to watch her come home every day. Our moms, on the other hand, waited at home, savoring each moment of silence before we burst through the doors. Lucy regularly invited kids to her house after school, and her mom always had delicious snacks awaiting our arrival. We never got bored at Lucy's house. Lucy's mom would join in our play and often came up with ideas for new games. Lucy was a dearly loved child, as all the second graders who knew her could see. Deep down I doubted that I was as dearly loved as Lucy.

Although Lucy and I lost touch when I went to a private school, I ran into her during adolescence. Her parents had divorced, and she was living in an apartment with her mom, whom she hated. She had started hanging out with a group of troubled kids, and she wasn't nearly as cute and put together as she had been in second grade. Perhaps her mother's lavish displays of love were an attempt to distract her from feeling lonely in a loveless marriage. Maybe what looked like "dearly loved" to me actually felt to Lucy like pressure to make her mom's life worthwhile. Seeing Lucy's condition made me reconsider my own parents and appreciate the ways they loved me.

Deep inside, we all want to be dearly loved children. One way you can spot someone who knows they are a dearly loved child of God is whether they do the same things God does. When you feel dearly loved by God, you want to be like Him!

My daughter is a teenager now, so she is appalled to know how much she wanted to be like me as a preschooler. I suppose I was the most fascinating woman she knew. Whatever I was doing, she wanted to do. She sat on the bathroom floor and watched me put on makeup. Now she hardly listens to my fashion advice, but back then she loved it when we wore matching clothes. I was writing a dissertation during those early years of her life, so even at age three, she had her own dissertation hot off the presses. Rachel literally delighted in me in response to how I delighted in her. The hallmark of intimacy with God is when you are so in love with Him that your deepest desire is to do what He does. You want to be just like your Daddy. You want to be like Him because you love Him.

Calling God "Daddy" is an experience of emotional closeness and connection to God. It happens in your spirit, as the Spirit of God testifies with your spirit that you are God's child and you cry out to your Abba-Daddy. Romans 8:15 says, "For you did not receive a spirit that makes you a slave again to fear, but you received the Spirit of sonship. And by him we cry, 'Abba, Father.'" Have you ever experienced the kind of emotional closeness with God that those verses describe? Has your spirit ever cried out, "Abba"? You won't cry out to Abba unless you know that you are a dearly loved child.

Your Daddy Has a Special Name for You

I really don't recall who decided my nickname. I have no idea how anyone would come up with this name for me. But when I was younger I was given a nickname known only to the insiders in my life. My parents, siblings, grandfather, and aunt used to call me this name. It was cute. It was sweet. Though endearing, I never wanted to hear it again after I was a teenager. It was my secret name. Revelation 2:17 promises me that I have another secret name. God writes this name on a white stone, and it is known only to God and myself. This is my precious and special name. I can't wait to know the name God chose for me. Just like I felt loved and special when I was called "Doodlebug" as a child, as God's child there will be a name only He calls me that helps me know how special I am to Him.

Your Daddy Sings over You

Zephaniah 3:17 says: "The LORD your God is with you, he is mighty to save. He will take great delight in you, he will quiet you with his love, he will rejoice over you with singing." I loved to sing to my babies. When they were infants they would rather hear me sing than Barbara Streisand any day. Singing to someone is an intimate encounter. When have you heard the Father singing over you? If you learn how to listen for His voice, you can enjoy His song as much as a newborn does her mother's lullabies.

My spiritual hearing may not be as sensitive as it could be, and I admit that I have never literally heard God singing over me with my human ears. I've tried to imagine just what He might sing. I didn't know God's repertoire, so I thought of the songs I enjoy singing to Him. I started with the first song I learned to sing, "Jesus Loves Me." I began to picture God singing similar words to me.

Debi loves Me, this I know
For her lifestyle tells Me so
Debi does to Me belong
She is weak, but I am strong
Yes, Debi loves Me
Yes, Debi loves Me
Yes, Debi loves Me
Her lifestyle tells Me so

The thought of God delighting in me like that blew my mind. Why don't you put this book down right now and ask God to help you think about the song He sings over you?

Your Daddy Favors You

Another way I sense His delight in me is when I realize that I have been the recipient of God's favor. We easily overlook the ways God delights in us. We look for spectacular, impressive ways for God to prove His love for us. We want big paychecks, fabulous trips, fame, and popularity before we will consider ourselves important to God. The truth is that most of the time when we are blessed like that, we don't even think about God.

Most of us grow out of our fascination with little gifts. I remember how excited and happy my children were when they were younger with the gifts we could afford to give them on Christmas morning. Now that they are older, Christmas is still fun, but the expression of wonder and delight is not the same.

The more intimate you grow with God, the more childlike you will become as you relish the little gifts He gives. Often God uses the little things to reveal how much He delights in us. A sunset can be a personal portrait created just to assure me that He loves me. Are you willing to experience God in the little things?

I try to help my children recognize God's favor. I hope my son Ben never forgets his fifth-grade derby car race. Building, painting, and racing derby cars is one of the tasks of a mission group at church. Ben was sick for several days and got behind on building his car. The day of the big race came, and his car didn't even have wheels. Fifteen minutes before the race, he asked his dad to help him hammer in the wheels. While they were hammering, a piece of the car broke off. They grabbed the Elmer's glue and bonded it back together. By the time it was Ben's turn to race, the glue was dry, but the car would only run on three wheels. Ben's friend worried and said, "Ben, you don't want to be the kid who comes in last." But what could he do? He took part in the race. He kept winning—maybe only three wheels touching made it faster! He came away with two trophies, one for first place in his grade level and one for second place all around. Who would have guessed?

More important than placing in a derby race, I hope Ben remembers how he was blessed by God. Savoring these experiences opens our souls to intimacy with God.

Have you seen God's favor on you? When did a sermon seem to be preached just to respond to the nagging dilemma you were experiencing? When has a passage of Scripture given you just the encouragement you needed? Intimacy is delighting in the little things. When was the last time you sat in the warmth of God's sunshine? Have you ever been enraptured with elation in God as you ponder His creation?

God Wants to Be Close to Us

One passage that best describes the intimacy I feel with God is Psalm 91:4: "He will cover you with his feathers, and under his wings you will find refuge." It reminds me of the heartfelt words Jesus spoke to the Pharisees the week before He died on the cross: "O Jerusalem, Jerusalem, you who kill the prophets and stone those sent to you, how often I have longed to gather your children together, as a hen gathers her chicks under her wings, but you were not willing" (Matt. 23:37).

God wants to hold you close. Without question, God is capable of entering into that kind of intimacy with you. His arms are wide open. His invitation has been offered. God wants to hold you and envelop you the way a mother bird protects her young.

Brian and I had the privilege of attending a spiritual retreat in England the week some Canadian goose goslings hatched at the retreat center. What a wonder to spy on the geese and observe their perceptive parenting skills. I must admit, I wasn't much of a goose admirer before. Their presence meant walking around distasteful piles of, shall we politely say, "goose waste." One retreat participant did testify that God spoke to her through the repulsive scene they created. She sensed God telling her that He was right with her in the mess and dung of her life and would show her the way to get out without stepping into the mess if she would follow His path. But I had simply considered them a nuisance and avoided any close proximity to the pond they called home.

One morning I was sitting yards away on a comfortable porch, watching, reflecting, and listening to God. My attention focused on the geese. Though I didn't admire them as housekeepers, I was quite in awe of them as parents. The geese were protective and proud, strutting their great miracle of four goslings around the pond for all to see. The six of them stuck together, the parents leading the way. Since the goslings were young, the morning coolness quickly got the best of them. Somehow the mother goose knew just the right time to call them back and gather them under her wings. The four little goslings would haphazardly run to their mother's wide-open wings, and as soon as they came, she would pull them in close, gently laying her wings over them. Still as a statue she would sit, patiently waiting for her little ones to be warmed in her care. She never seemed bored, she never seemed distracted, and she seemed quite content to keep her little ones close in a sacred embrace.

This is what Jesus longs to do for us. He knows we are cold, some of us even freezing, from the effects of a harsh, cruel world. He knows we need a reprieve from the pain and agony. He spreads His wings wide to cover us and provide the warmth we need. There is only one condition: we have to be willing.

One thing is for certain—you can never know the wonder of an intimate relationship with God unless you are willing. It's not like a kiss from Aunt Gertrude. Everyone has an aunt like her. She lives to be reunited with family so she can pull her unsuspecting eight-year-old nephew into her arms, bring him close to her soft, cushioned body, and plant a big, wet kiss right on his lips. It's disgustingly familiar. Jesus never embraces that way. He never grabs you and pulls you close against your will. He only opens wide His arms to you and offers to warm you under the shelter of His wings. Are you willing to come?

Closeness to God Is the Antidote to Loneliness

One of the greatest human dilemmas is the anguish of loneliness. Fear of loneliness is the driving force behind many decisions we make in life, positive or negative.

Roger's wife of twenty-five years died of breast cancer. The year they discovered her cancer, Roger and Karen were the happiest they had ever been in their marriage. They had weathered many of the normal storms and crises of marriage—teenagers, financial problems, miscarriages—and they came back stronger than ever. For years they had dedicated themselves to work as elders for a new church plant. Their two girls were grown, one married, and their life together had begun to revolve around themselves as a couple again. Life was good. Their marriage was good. But when Karen died, Roger found himself drowning in his grief and loneliness.

A loneliness he had never known in his busy, active life overpowered and consumed him. But you wouldn't know it from watching Roger. Two years after losing Karen, he appeared to be doing fine. In fact, he became busier than ever, taking frequent mission trips with his church. He looked like someone who had clearly dealt with his grief and was moving on.

Inside, his soul was ravished with pain, hurt, and grief. He took mission trips not to serve God but to try to escape the memories. The problem was, nothing worked. No amount of work, trips around the world, dinner with friends, or dates with great women could take away the searing emotional pain, the sickening heaviness that was his chronic companion. Every day he would wake up hoping that enough time had passed. Perhaps this day would be different. But every morning it was still there—a loneliness that wouldn't go away.

Roger was acutely in touch with his loneliness. Are you? Blaise Pascal spoke of this place inside each of us as the God-shaped vacuum only God can fill. That's the place that is longing for a Daddy-God relationship. It's the place your heart cries out for something more. You have a hidden place in your soul that is desperately longing for the love of God.

God wants to give you something more that you need, and that something is emotional closeness with Him. In my work as a counselor I had a window into other people's experience of loneliness. Panic disorders, depression, eating disorders, and other issues often have fear and loneliness as their source. People explained how they felt desperate whether living in a house full of family or by themselves.

Loneliness isn't about having people around you. The abyss of loneliness is meant to be filled with God alone. People can distract you from your loneliness, but they can't touch or fill that part of you. That is the place that is longing for intimacy with God.

When God created Adam and Eve, He met with them in the Garden of Eden. They would walk together and enjoy the universe. A place inside you wants to walk with God too. It is the place that feels lonely, insecure, and unsure of why you exist. Only God can fix this place. Here's an excerpt from my journal that describes how God filled my loneliness.

Just now my travel plans have been delayed by five hours. My fellow travelers and I hate this experience that is disrupting our lives and changing our plans. These hours have given me an unexpected opportunity to connect with God.

Though I sit in the airport a stranger in this town, I'm not bored or out of touch. I am here with God. I'm more attentive to Him than I would be had my plans gone as I wanted. Instead of being home and back into my crazy, hectic life, I've got some extra time to be with God, undisturbed.

I'm even surprising myself with how agreeable I am to this unexpected derailment. Rather than cursing the plan, I settle in and consider that God is the God of the universe, so He could easily fix a plane and make us all happy. But evidently that isn't His plan. And it causes me to remember. I remember that this change in plans gives me a renewed sense of what it means to be emotionally close to God.

I'm not alone. I didn't need to frantically buy a magazine or talk to a stranger. I can be with God. I can delight in His presence.

The change in my plans was used to remind me that Christ is in charge of this universe. It gave me hope. I decided to be thankful for this fact and that He knows more than I do.

Closeness to God Is a Delightful Experience

The Gospels tell us that Jesus spent entire nights with God in prayer. The thought of praying all night is foreign to most of us. We can hardly imagine how Jesus could have done it. Many of us struggle to spend fifteen minutes in prayer. And not only did Jesus spend such a long time in prayer, He missed sleep to spend time with God.

I don't miss sleep for much. I'm one of those who needs eight hours a night. I can regularly be found taking a thirty-minute nap. Sleep is important to me. The only time in my life that I missed sleep for thirty-six hours straight was the night my daughter was born. I checked into the hospital at midnight, and she came into the world at 3:29 a.m. By the time the world was informed that she was here, morning had come. In spite of all my body had been through, I couldn't possibly close my eyes to rest. I was so enraptured with my new baby that sleep didn't even cross my mind until hours later.

I imagine that those feelings are similar to the way Jesus felt when He gave up sleep to spend time with God. He was so enraptured with being in God's presence that time or sleep didn't seem to matter.

Imagine yourself feeling that way about being with God. I bet you would be able to delay sleep if you were with someone you admired. You may remember not caring about time or sleep when you spent an evening with good friends. The enjoyment and conversation were so powerful, you didn't look at your watch until it was way past midnight. That's the kind of feeling that Jesus had in His relationship with God. Isn't that the kind of relationship you want with God? You can feel that way about being with Him.

The apostle Paul was obsessed with God. He wanted people to be single, like him, so they could serve God without distraction from family obligations (1 Cor. 7:8). He said that for him to live is Christ (Phil. 1:21). He couldn't wait to be reunited with Christ (Phil. 1:23). You don't have to be single to have the kind of single-minded focus on loving God that Paul had. Paul fully enjoyed being able to have an intimate connection with God. Many believers have shared his enthusiasm. I recommend you read the biographies of well-known Christians to inspire you on your journey.

You Can Claim God as Your Father

Have you known the compassion of a father? Even if you haven't, you can still know the compassion of God as Father. Let yourself enter into His heart of love for you. I guarantee you that seeing God's compassionate Father's heart for you will change your prayer life. It will even help you embrace the hard parts of your journey.

Psalm 68:5 says that God is a father to the fatherless. In a sense we are all fatherless. My father is a good man. He is faithful to God and seeks to do right. But my father does not meet all my needs. My relationship with him reveals how much more I need than he can give me. He gave me a home and paid for my education, but he cannot give me security and hope.

God knows the fatherless need a father. God knows you need a father too, and He wants to be that for you. Isaiah 9:6 says, "And he will be called Wonderful Counselor, Mighty God, Everlasting Father, Prince of Peace." Among the names that Jesus would be called are the words *Everlasting Father*. A place in your soul needs an Everlasting Father. Your hunger for a father cannot be completely met by your earthly dad.

Second Corinthians 6:18 reminds us that what God told David in 2 Samuel 7:14 is true for us: "I will be a Father to you, and you will be my sons and daughters, says the Lord Almighty." You must stop looking to your earthly father so you can let God become your Father. When you do, you will find yourself wanting to defend your Father-God's honor.

Knowing God as Father Provokes Deep Loyalty

Jesus was vigilant about His Father's desires. When He threw the money changers out of the temple court in a violent outburst, His rationale was that His Father's house was to be a house of prayer (John 2:13–16). How do you feel when God's name is being misused? Do you have that same kind of loyalty to God?

We see Jesus's loyalty when He cried, "Father, forgive them" (Luke 23:34). He knew His Father's heart was crushed to see His own Son being rejected and abused. Jesus's death on the cross was just as tormenting for His Father as it was for Jesus. Yet both desperately wanted to restore their relationship with humanity and knew there was no other way, so they went through it for us.

During the most difficult moment in His life, Jesus called to His Father for help. He prayed, "Father, if you are willing, take this cup from me" (Luke 22:42). Even when God could not take the cup (dying on the cross), Jesus remained loyal to God.

He chose loyalty to His Father's plan rather than trying to find another way.

Emotional closeness between you and God is pictured in a father-child relationship. Is that what you are experiencing with God? Psalm 103:13–14 compares the compassion a father has for his child to the compassion God has for you. Do you feel connected to God like a child does to his dad? A good father disciplines his son. Since God is the best Father, He doesn't spare us from discipline. We will discover how important testing is in building our intimacy with God.

Reflection Questions:

1. How do you sense God delighting in you?
2. What song do you imagine God singing over you?
3. When have you felt closest to God?
4. How does God want to fill your loneliness?
5. How do you try to fill your loneliness apart from God?
6. Are you still fatherless, or have you claimed God as your true Father?

Intimacy Exercise:

Set aside thirty minutes to connect with God. You can take a walk or just sit in a comfortable place. Determine in your heart, soul, and mind that these thirty minutes are to be focused solely on being with God. Listen to God speaking to you about what you are seeing, feeling, and experiencing. Watch ants, notice sounds, discern what God may be telling you about yourself. Open your Bible and read Scripture, or let God remind you about Scripture you have memorized. You may want to journal what you experience.

9 The Discipline of Intimacy

My son, do not despise the LORD's discipline and do not resent his rebuke, because the LORD disciplines those he loves, as a father the son he delights in.

Proverbs 3:11–12

One of the worst places to meet an undisciplined child is on a cross-country plane trip. Being confined with this kind of child on a plane will lead anyone to question their own parenting strategies. One conclusion you might consider is whether an undisciplined child is a loved child. How could you raise a child to be despised by a whole planeload of passengers if you really loved him? God proves His love for us by disciplining us.

God Has Expectations of His Children

Part of knowing God as Father is accepting that a good father disciplines his children. Hebrews 12:5–6 explains: "And you have forgotten that word of encouragement that addresses you as sons:

'My son, do not make light of the Lord's discipline, and do not lose heart when he rebukes you, because the Lord disciplines those he loves, and he punishes everyone he accepts as a son.'" A good daddy has expectations of his children. He encourages us to reach our personal potential.

Don't get me wrong; God isn't the kind of parent who insists on straight A's for every child. He does want each of us to reach his full potential. He has set a personal best and He wants us to achieve it.

Our son, Ben, has dyslexia. This reality does not set him up to have the kind of instant success our daughter Rachel has with school. Her optimal learning style is the way schools teach. My husband and I don't expect Ben to learn in the exact way our daughter does. We do expect him to learn! He might be tempted to compare himself with her and think, *I can't make straight A's, so why try?* This kind of thinking is not acceptable to us.

Instead we have taught him about the unique way God has designed his brain. We celebrate the intelligence he has that often goes unrecognized on a spelling test. We encourage him to understand that God has gifted him with dyslexia. It helps him see the world in a way that others miss. God and we (his parents) expect him to learn to his full potential. First Peter 1:17 says, "Since you call on a Father who judges each man's work impartially, live your lives as strangers here in reverent fear." Like God, we consider our children's individuality when we discipline them about their work at school.

The Gospels of Matthew and Luke contain Jesus's parable of the talents (Matt. 25:14–30; Luke 19:12–27). This story illustrates God's desire that we give Him our personal best. It shows clearly that God will not accept excuses for not achieving what He destined for us.

Jesus told how a master went away on a trip. Before he left, he gave five talents (a talent was an amount of money equal to more than one thousand dollars) to one servant, two talents to another, and one to a third servant. When he returned he discovered that the servant who had been given five talents now had ten. The one who had been given two had doubled his as well. But the servant who had been given one had hidden it out of fear of the master. The master was very displeased with this servant and gave his one talent to the servant who had ten. Jesus was teaching that God wants us to use what He has given us for His glory. He knows we aren't all a Moses or a Daniel or a Job. But we each have spiritual gifts and resources which He expects us to be using for His glory.

God Tests His Children

If you hang out with Jesus long enough, a time will come when you will be tested. Jesus isn't trying to make you fail; He wants to make sure you really understand who He is and what your relationship with Him is all about. These tests will come in big ways and small.

In Deuteronomy 8:2 Moses reminded the Israelites of the way God tested them before his death: "Remember how the LORD your God led you all the way in the desert these forty years, to humble you and to test you in order to know what was in your heart, whether or not you would keep his commands." Because the Israelites didn't trust God would take them into the Promised Land when He brought them out of Egypt, God used forty years of wandering in the wilderness to test and discipline them. If you read the book of Joshua you will discover that God's discipline worked.

Jesus taught many important lessons to the disciples. These were the guys who had a lot of work to do after Jesus left the earth. Jesus's job was redeeming the world. He left the disciples and the rest of us the responsibility for carrying out God's plan by spreading His message. So Jesus had to be certain His disciples were getting it. He needed to test them occasionally. The disciples didn't know that Jesus was planning a pop quiz that day. If they had, maybe they would have prepared. Maybe they would have quickly reviewed their notes, remembering the power He had to heal fatal diseases and all the amazing truths He had been teaching. The disciples didn't fare very well on this test, recorded in John 6.

Jesus had been teaching on a mountain. Crowds had followed Him there because they wanted to be a part of the miracles and signs that Jesus was performing. They were so caught up in the wonder of Jesus that they forgot about their to-do list for the day—most didn't even take time to pack a lunch; they just got up and followed.

Jesus knew this problem would create a teachable moment. John 6:5–6 explains: "When Jesus looked up and saw a great crowd coming toward him, he said to Philip, 'Where shall we buy bread for these people to eat?' He asked this only to test him, for he already had in mind what he was going to do." It was time for a little pop quiz. How much had the disciples learned about Jesus so far?

Philip chose the most obvious wrong answer: "Do you have any idea how much it would cost to serve this many people? And where could we possibly get it?" Andrew piped up with a half-hearted guess: "Here's a little boy with a lunch, but it won't begin to feed the crowd." He was getting closer to the right answer.

Jesus didn't shame them for their wrong answers. He simply showed them what the right answer was. He asked their help in getting everyone to sit down in an organized fashion. Then He blessed the little boy's lunch and gave out enough food for over five thousand.

Have you ever stopped and wondered what the right answer to Jesus's test question was? "Where shall we buy food for these people to eat?" The right answer is, "Heaven only knows." The disciples were getting ready for some major exams in the future. They needed to learn to think outside the box, to realize that God doesn't always use the obvious. Have you passed that test?

How do you respond when Jesus tests you? I know I often react like Philip. I get an assignment from God and consider it impossible, so I question God's sanity. I think God has lost touch with how hard it is down here. This earth just can't take another war or another untimely death. I wonder if He really knows best when there is so much pain and suffering. It doesn't take a thought that noble for me to become indignant against God, either. Sometimes I can be that way just because my own life seems to hit a rough spot. I have more bills than money to pay them. My child is sick and I can't figure out why. I feel too much pressure to get things finished. A simple thing like stubbing my toe can get me all bent out of shape thinking God doesn't care or give me what I need. Other times, I'm like Andrew and look only at the resources I have.

One of the subjects God has tested me on is forgiveness. I remember experiencing a huge hurt and taking about two years to break free from the trap of bitterness. That happened early in my adulthood. It wasn't a once-in-a-lifetime test. Since then I've been asked to forgive that same person and many others.

In the end, forgiveness is a test of my love and trust in God. My human reason tells me to seek revenge, or at least not to have any kind of relationship with someone who offends me. God asks me to trust Him to take care of my enemies.

God Disciplines Us for a Reason

God disciplines us to help us grow in a personal relationship with Him in the future. His discipline has a purpose. Our children sometimes doubt our rationale for discipline. Sometimes

I do the same to God. He disciplines me to help me become the woman I want to be. Without discipline I could not be that woman.

Even nature exposes the importance of discipline for growth. The Biosphere2 is an experiment outside Tucson, Arizona, that replicates various earth systems. When it was first designed they did not replicate wind. The result was plants that grew large and quickly, but fell over. "It was determined that the lack of wind created trees with much softer wood than the species would normally make in the wild. They grew more quickly than they did in the wild, but they were harmed in the long run as a consequence."[1]

Eliphaz was one of Job's counselors who totally misinterpreted the events of Job's life. However, the way he explained God in Job 5:17–22 was accurate: "Blessed is the man whom God corrects; so do not despise the discipline of the Almighty" (v. 17). Have you been disciplined by the Almighty? If you have, you are blessed. God only disciplines the son He loves (Prov. 3:12). Being disciplined by God is not rejection but evidence that He claims you as His child.

Job 5:18 says, "For he wounds, but he also binds up; he injures, but his hands also heal." God never wounds us without hope of healing us. I love the way this verse points out that God's own hands are what heal us. He does discipline, wound, or injure us, but only because we need it. He always heals through His hands, His touch.

I've got to say I think our God tends to be remarkably lenient. I know God has been incredibly lenient with me. I also see it in the way He dealt with the nation of Israel in the Old Testament. Some people avoid reading the Old Testament because they think the Old Testament God is cruel. If they took the time to really read it, they would discover how patient and slow to anger God is. The Israelites consistently disobeyed God, ignored Him, and worshiped other gods, but God was completely faithful to the promises He made in His covenant. God is incredibly patient and kind as He disciplines us.

The only reason God disciplines us is to help us develop the faith we need to follow Him. Life is made sweeter by hard work and determination. Some children of affluent parents are at greater risk for drug abuse and other counterproductive behaviors. When children are given everything they could ever want, it is not satisfying. Spiritual discipline works in the same manner: waiting and watching develops your character. Romans 5:3–4 says: "Not only so, but we also rejoice in our sufferings, because we know that suffering produces perseverance; perseverance, character; and character, hope."

We need to learn how to look at our suffering the way Jesus did. First Peter 4:1–2 says, "Therefore, since Christ suffered in his body, arm yourselves also with the same attitude, because he who has suffered in his body is done with sin. As a result, he does not live the rest of his earthly life for human desires, but rather for the will of God." How can you have joy when you are going through hard times? If you experience your hardships connected to God as Daddy, you will gain a totally different understanding of suffering. If you stop thinking, *God must hate me because these hard things are happening to me*, and start thinking, *God must have a purpose for everything that happens in my life*, you will find joy in suffering.

Discipline Works

Like it or not, most of us have experienced the greatest spiritual growth in times of affliction. J. C. Ryle says, "Through affliction He teaches us many precious lessons that otherwise we would never learn. By affliction He shows us our emptiness and weakness, draws us to the throne of grace, purifies our affections, weans us from the world, and makes us long for heaven."[2] Whether our afflictions come purposely from the hand of God or whether He simply uses them as opportunities for growth, they have purpose in our life and in increasing our love and trust of God.

Hebrews 12:7–11 explains God's purposes in affliction:

Endure hardship as discipline; God is treating you as sons. For what son is not disciplined by his father? If you are not disciplined (and everyone undergoes discipline), then you are illegitimate children and not true sons. Moreover, we have all had human fathers who disciplined us and we respected them for it. How much more should we submit to the Father of our spirits and live! Our fathers disciplined us for a little while as they thought best; but God disciplines us for our good, that we may share in his holiness. No discipline seems pleasant at the time, but painful. Later on, however, it produces a harvest of righteousness and peace for those who have been trained by it.

The issues on which I choose to discipline my children are what I think are most important to help them become successful in life. I am basically making an educated guess when I discipline. I base my decisions on the things that helped me become successful, my knowledge of child development, and the Bible. I hope that I am disciplining my children in a good way that will bring about the best in life for them, but I can't make the same guarantee God does about His discipline. He says that His discipline and every hardship we endure will produce righteousness and peace in us. It is a sure thing.

Do You See the Value in Your Hardships?

I remember a time when I was helping some seventh graders during a Jigsaw Jamboree. They were divided in teams of four to five and were racing against each other to put together a five-hundred-piece jigsaw puzzle. One of the groups was at a standstill. A girl complained to me that their puzzle was defective. After she put together all the outer edge pieces, the sides were not even. The helpers were instructed not to give direct advice to the students, so I asked, "Suppose your puzzle wasn't defective. What could the problem be?" The girl took a minute to look at her puzzle again, and soon she figured out which side had too many pieces, which had too few, and what was necessary to fix the problem.

Too many times we blame God when our lives aren't running as smoothly as we expect. Like Job, we think somehow God has made a mistake (Job 40:2). Perhaps if we look at who God says He is and not at our circumstances to define who He is, we will get a more accurate picture. We need to be like those seventh graders and take another look at our lives. We need to look from the perspective that since God is not defective, maybe something about our lives and relationship with God needs a second look.

Do you need a clearer understanding that God disciplines the sons He loves? Proverbs 3:11–12 says one of the ways God loves us is by disciplining us: "My son, do not despise the LORD's discipline and do not resent his rebuke, because the LORD disciplines those he loves, as a father the son he delights in." Love, delight, and discipline are interrelated. Love and delight implies discipline, because without discipline we are not loved and delighted in—we are ignored. Being ignored by a parent doesn't give a child a sense of self-respect and love. If God loves you enough to die for you, you can be sure that He loves you enough to discipline you.

Jesus told us, "How much more shall your Father which is in heaven give good things to them that ask him!" (Matt. 7:11). You've got to realize that any hard or difficult situation you face is known by God. He can use it for your good.

Oswald Chambers explained it this way: "There are times, says Jesus, when God cannot lift the darkness from you, but trust Him. God will appear like an unkind friend, but He is not; He will appear like an unnatural Father, but He is not; He will appear like an unjust judge, but He is not. Keep the notion of the mind of God behind all things strong and growing."[3] God is watching the way we respond to every trial. James 1:12 says, "Blessed is the man who perseveres under trial, because when he has stood the test, he will receive the crown of life that God has promised to those who love him." Every hardship you endure for God's glory will be rewarded in heaven.

God Suffers

During the news coverage of the war in Iraq, I heard a muscular marine comment on the torture that then nineteen-year-old Jessica Lynch suffered as a POW. In the wake of her daring rescue, this marine stated, "I admire her for living through this. I'm six foot three. I'm a big guy, and she's only about five foot two. I don't know if I could have made it." When we think of Jesus's physical suffering, we have a similar sentiment. We can imagine what it would be like to feel the stress He felt in the garden when His sweat turned to blood. We cringe when we think about the beatings and the pain from thorns poking into His skull. We feel the horror of His back being lacerated by a Roman whip. We can imagine the pain of nails entering through His wrist and exiting to the other side. We can understand the agony of the suffocation on the cross. Each of these thoughts deepens our appreciation of what Jesus did for us through His suffering. We think, *I don't know if I could have done that.*

Do you ever stop to think that God suffered when Jesus died on the cross for our sin? God the Father, God the Son, and God the Holy Spirit suffered. They suffer as they work to bring about our redemption. They suffer because some people they love will not be able to join them in heaven. They suffer when they see the suffering that we go through.

I had a short experience of being exposed to the way God suffers. I was visiting a Dallas museum with a group of school-children. This particular week they had an exhibit of Pulitzer Prize–winning photographs. (The children were not required to look at this exhibit.) I soon discovered that the subjects of Pulitzer Prize–winning photographs are often human misery. One showed a starving baby left for dead in an African desert with a vulture nearby. Others were pictures of executions and victims of natural disasters. I only viewed part of the exhibit before I had to walk away. I didn't want to see any more. I'd had enough! Then I thought about God. I realized He sees this kind of human tragedy every day, every moment, and He doesn't turn away, even though it breaks His heart.

Our suffering is due to sin as well. God did not create us to suffer. Suffering began when we doubted God's goodness. Until both Adam and Eve ate from the Tree of Knowledge of Good and Evil, suffering didn't exist. As soon as Adam finished his bite, the torture of shame, self-doubt, and rejection erupted within the once-perfect universe. It caused suffering for us as well as God.

Discipline Shows Us What We Are Really Made Of

Hebrews 5:7–9 tells us about Jesus's experience with suffering:

During the days of Jesus' life on earth, he offered up prayers and petitions with loud cries and tears to the one who could save him from death, and he was heard because of his reverent submission. Although he was a son, he learned obedience from what he suffered and, once made perfect, he became the source of eternal salvation for all who obey him.

Jesus suffered. He was suffering when He offered up prayers and petitions with loud cries and tears to the one who could save Him from death. I've never prayed better than when I'm in pain. Nothing distracts me from prayer when I am praying like that. Like Jesus's prayers, my prayers during suffering are loud cries. I encourage you to do this in your hard times. Offer prayers and requests with loud cries and tears to the God you believe is good to you.

Next, like Jesus, you need to submit to God. Jesus's submission was called a reverent submission. His obedience in suffering enabled Him to become the source of eternal salvation for all who will obey Him. He was perfect. Yet it was only through suffering that He received what He and His Father wanted most—relationship with humankind! Don't think for a minute that God doesn't know what you are going through. He is more deeply acquainted with suffering than you could ever imagine!

In the midst of discipline or testing, we realize how much we love and trust God. Such struggles are mandatory for our maturity. We would never develop the faith we are going to need without periods of discipline and testing.

God tested Abraham by asking him to offer his long-awaited and much-loved son Isaac as a human sacrifice. Abraham passed with flying colors and made God proud (Gen. 22:1–18). God tested the Israelites to see if they would follow His instructions when He sent them bread from heaven. Many passed that test, but some of them failed and ended up with a pail of smelly maggots (Exod. 16:4, 20). Jesus tested the disciples when He asked them where they should get food to feed a large crowd (John 6:5–6). The disciples ended up bungling the test, but Jesus applied a curve and they passed in the end.

You too will be tested along your spiritual journey. How will you do? Let's look in the next chapter at how this journey and testing continues throughout our time on earth.

Reflection Questions:

1. Why does a good father discipline his son?
2. What kind of expectations does a good father have for his children?
3. Why does God discipline us?
4. What did Jesus focus on when He faced suffering?
5. How does discipline show us what we are made of?
6. How do you score on God's tests so far in your life?

Intimacy Exercise:

Make a list of the tests you have been given throughout your spiritual life. By each one write whether you passed or failed.

10 The Journey of Intimacy

For he chose us in him before the creation of the world to be
holy and blameless in his sight. In love he predestined us to be
adopted as his sons through Jesus Christ, in accordance with
his pleasure and will.

Ephesians 1:4–5

In college my goal was preparing to be the best Christian counselor I could be. I decided that doing my job well would require a
thorough knowledge of God's Word so that I would have God's
answers to the problems people face. I imagined myself in the
future as a wise woman sitting in her office, encouraging others
through the Scriptures. I never sat down and made plans to accomplish this goal. I don't remember contemplating a specific
program to memorize certain verses or outline the Bible. I just
knew that knowing God's Word was what it would take to be
an effective counselor.

I spent eighteen years as a Christian counselor before God
called me to become a women's minister. It dawned on me that
I do have a powerful knowledge of God's Word. I share this
knowledge with those who come into my office. Many times

what I have to share with others is something God has shown me just that day or week in my personal devotional time or what I have been taught at church. Often I know what is contained in a Scripture passage just by seeing the reference. When I'm listening to someone speak from God's Word, my mind floods with teachings from my long history of being acquainted with that same passage. I am equipped in the Word to help people. It is a good feeling. It is a positive revelation.

I recognize that other people acknowledge my expertise in God's Word and how to apply it to the struggles people face. They see it as a sign of maturity. I like being seen this way. I like feeling this way. I even sense that God is proud of me. I don't doubt that my self-glorification is a concern to Him, but it also brings Him great pleasure that I have obeyed His instructions and have experienced such blessing as a result. Realizing my knowledge gave me the feeling of success, that somehow I had made it. I had arrived at a spiritual goal that I vaguely made for myself.

Recognizing our successes is good. Celebrating spiritual growth is important. You should be able to see progress on your spiritual journey. But you need to know something about this progress. Be aware that spiritual intimacy is not an event; it is a process. It happens in a continuous spiral, shaped like a funnel. You continue to move through the cycle we have studied. The journey around the cycle gets smaller and smaller as you draw closer to God.

When I first started growing as a Christian, I became discouraged that I wasn't making the progress I thought I would. I guess I believed that a time would come in my Christian experience when I would reach a certain spiritual state and would never struggle again. I would be through with sinning. I would make it and never have to worry about falling back. That was not what happened.

I remember talking to my youth minister about this. He explained that if Christian growth could be charted on a graph, it would include ups and downs. The ups and downs happen regularly. He told me that in a healthy Christian life, over time the downs are not as far down and the ups are higher. Actually, when you step back and take in the whole picture, you can see upward movement. I found his advice to be true. I've been a Christian for over thirty years now, and this has consistently been my experience.

I have shared in this book what I have observed in my own life. My growth seems to happen in this cycle. I don't believe I will get off the cycle until heaven, but I do feel closer to God each time I journey through it. I offer this cycle to help you envision the journey. Nothing is new, innovative, or magical about this cycle. It is simply what I have identified as the pivotal and familiar places on my journey to the heart of God. Many spiritual writers have shared their perspective of the development of spiritual maturity. My prayer is that what I share would speak to others in a way that draws them close to God.

I have noticed that just because I go through brokenness and it results in deep Abba-Father, Daddy-God experiences doesn't make me immune from future brokenness. The difference is that I learn to cry, "Abba, Father!" sooner in my brokenness. Thus the cycle is repeated, but with more intimate results and quicker flow through the cycle, which gives it the shape of a narrowing funnel.

My children were coming of age just as the chicken pox vaccine was emerging. When Rachel got chicken pox at age four, doctors weren't even giving the vaccine to children on a regular basis, and since it was made from human blood, we opted not to consider it further. Four years later, many parents were volunteering to have a chicken pox vaccine given to their children. Medicine had advanced and the vaccine was becoming more widely used. Brian and I decided that we wouldn't get the vaccine for our son Ben since at that time doctors weren't sure when a booster would be needed. We had already been through the disease with our daughter, and although it was unpleasant, the lifetime immunity that was guaranteed as a result of enduring the pain of chicken pox seemed worthwhile to us.

You don't get lifetime immunity from future brokenness when you work through the cycle of intimacy with God. You do receive lifetime benefits resulting from that brokenness. Although you won't automatically have instant peace through all difficult experiences, you might notice that the same things don't create the degree of pain and brokenness they did in the past.

I recently talked to a man who was almost shocked that he didn't feel angry at God when he lost his job for the fifth time in six years. The previous four times, lashing out at God was his first response. This time, he started to lash out at God but stopped himself, knowing that God didn't deserve his anger and that connecting with God was the only way he could get through a challenge like this. That is definitely one of the marks of growth. He isn't immune from future brokenness, but past brokenness made a difference in how he experienced his present brokenness.

Oswald Chambers says, "Either Jesus Christ is a deceiver and Paul is deluded, or some extraordinary thing happens to a man who holds on to the love of God when the odds are against God's character."[1] This is the mark of spiritual growth. We come to a point when we do not use the logic of our circumstances to dictate our knowledge of God. Paul asked in Romans 8:35, "Who can separate us from the love of Christ?" His answer was that nothing we can experience on Earth or in heaven can separate us from Christ's love. One of the evidences that you really know how to love God as your Father is that when you are struggling through difficult times, you refuse to judge God on the basis of your circumstances.

You know you are getting it when you don't doubt the goodness of God. You are discovering the amazing depths of a relationship with God that allows you to cry out, "Abba, Father," as Jesus did on that night of utter terror in His soul. The prophet Habakkuk said,

> Though the fig tree does not bud and there are no grapes on the vines, though the olive crop fails and the fields produce no food, though there are no sheep in the pen and no cattle in the stalls, yet I will rejoice in the LORD, I will be joyful in God my Savior. The Sovereign LORD is my strength; he makes my feet like the feet of a deer, he enables me to go on the heights.
>
> Habakkuk 3:17–19

Those words are the goal of each of us on the journey of intimacy with God.

The Cycle of Pressing On

Paul describes the process we are discussing so well in Philippians 3:12: "Not that I have already obtained all this, or have already been made perfect, but I press on to take hold of that for which Christ Jesus took hold of me."

My extended family still reflects on the Arkansas vacation we shared many years ago. It produced one of those moments that you had to be there to fully appreciate and created an inside phrase that we all fondly remember. We had a wonderful time on a wilderness ranch complete with the charms of country living, especially the caretaker. He came promptly before checkout to "settle up" before we headed home. My dad was taking care of the bill. The caretaker sat down at the kitchen counter, calculator in hand. He seemed to be off in his own little world, and my dad, ready to pay his bill and get on the road, had to prompt him back to reality by asking what was owed. "Well," the caretaker started in his southern drawl, "the cabin charge is. . . ." My dad replied, "And what about the additional people?" "Ain't got there yet" was the caretaker's instant reply. My dad would attempt to give the caretaker ample time to figure the sum, but each time he prodded with a question, the caretaker responded, "Ain't got there yet." None of us felt my dad was rushing him, and the caretaker wasn't angry or anxious; he simply was on Arkansas time when it came to figuring up a bill. Now when any of us find ourselves being rushed by each other, we respond, "Ain't got there yet." We all relax and have a little chuckle.

I think Paul would like that phrase and understand its meaning, especially when it comes to spirituality. We simply "ain't got there yet." You need to relax and be okay with this fact. You ain't got there yet, and you won't be there yet until you reach heaven and your redemption is complete. You need to settle in, chuckle, and wait.

One of the secrets to waiting to get there is found in Philippians 3:13–14. "Brothers, I do not consider myself yet to have taken hold of it. But one thing I do: forgetting what is behind and straining toward what is ahead, I press on." Don't let the accuser of the brethren, also known as Satan (Rev. 12:10), keep you stuck on all the things you should have done or known better than to be involved in. Keep going. Keep on keeping on in the freedom that there is no condemnation for those who are in Christ (Rom. 8:1).

Your Christian life is like a race. You keep moving closer to Jesus. He is the prize. You want to keep moving through the cycle of growing closer to Jesus in confidence that you are making spiritual progress—even though you ain't got there yet.

You Will Arrive

If you are like me, you might look back over your Christian life and feel ashamed that you haven't progressed further and been more victorious over Satan. Why are you still sinning? Why haven't the moments of knowing God as Father totally transformed your mind, body, and soul to the point that you are like Jesus?

Don't discount what you have experienced and how far you have come with God just because you still sin. A strong spiritual force is working against the intimacy God wants you to know in your relationship with Him. We are assured that a day will come when Satan will be taken care of. The book of Revelation prophesies the complete end of Satan's influence on the world. Why hasn't it happened yet? What could God be thinking?

John Piper asked the question, "Why is Satan left on earth?" He offers this thought:

The key is that God aims to defeat Satan in a way that glorifies not only his power, but also the superior beauty and worth and desirability of his Son over Satan. God could simply exert raw power and snuff Satan out. That would glorify God's power. But it would not display so clearly the superior worth of Jesus over Satan. That will be displayed as Christ defeats Satan by his death and then by winning superior allegiance from the saints over the lies of Satan.[2]

Has Christ won superior allegiance over the lies of Satan in your life? That is what knowing God as Father is all about. The problems of this universe are never far from the heart of God. He is grieved by every painful situation we encounter. Yet He didn't end the world when it was devastated by sin. Instead, He revealed the opportunity we have to defeat sin through the power of Jesus Christ.

You Can Trust God as Father

The spiritual journey is about trusting God to do something glorious through us. Our natural instinct is to look for proof that we are not good enough. We doubt that we could be loved by God as by a papa. Fight that thought! As sinful as we are, God still loves us and longs to hold us close. Knowing God as Father is not contingent on being sinless. It is dependent on our willingness to accept our need for mercy and reconciliation with Him.

Remember the story Jesus told about the prodigal son? That son is you. You will leave the home of your heavenly Father more than once in your life. At times you will find yourself lost and depleted of spiritual resources. Suddenly you will remember how it felt to sit on the Father's lap, cuddle up, and call Him Dad. You too will come to your senses and return home to your Father. You will be received home if you come home with all your heart.

Knowing God as Father makes you want to be a better person. A line from the movie *As Good As It Gets* demonstrates this motivation to change. Jack Nicholson plays a successful novelist suffering from obsessive-compulsive disorder. He does not take his medication because of the side effects. He keeps everyone in his world at a distance because of his obsessive, mean, and controlling behaviors. Something happens when he forms a relationship with a waitress from a restaurant he frequents. During a date, which is not going well, he tries to explain how much he cares for her. She is agitated by his behavior but gives him a chance to share from his heart. He tells her about his medication and that he never takes it. Then he explains that since he's met her, he's started taking his medication. He says to her, "You make me want to be a better man."[3]

This is what happens to me as I respond to the invitation to know God as Father: I want to be a better person. He makes me better. I once heard a minister explain that the act of baptism is actually believing that we are better than we are. It is identifying with Christ's purity. When I was baptized I was saying, "I'm really better than I appear because of what Christ has done in me through my belief in Him." Peter explained it this way: "Since you call on a Father who judges each man's work impartially, live your lives as strangers here in reverent fear. For you know that it was not with perishable things such as silver or gold that you were redeemed from the empty way of life handed down to you from your forefathers, but with the precious blood of Christ, a lamb without blemish or defect" (1 Peter 1:17–19).

God didn't create something outside Himself in order to redeem us from Satan. He bought us with the precious blood of His own Son, His own self. I know that I will never comprehend the full extent of God's love for me. But I do want to thank Him for the part I do understand. I want to please Him with my life. I want to stop sinning because I have been so deeply loved.

The Response of a Grateful Heart

Those who have known God as Father are forever changed. They are not perfect, but they are different. A grateful heart is the outcome of knowing God as Father. Colossians 1:12 talks about "giving thanks to the Father, who has qualified you to share in the inheritance of the saints in the kingdom of light." When you accept God as Dad, He qualifies you to share in the great inheritance that is waiting for you in your future with Him.

Galatians 4:6–7 further explains: "Because you are sons, God sent the Spirit of his Son into our hearts, the Spirit who calls out, 'Abba, Father.' So you are no longer a slave, but a son; and since you are a son, God has made you also an heir." Don't forget that intimacy with God helps you not only in your life now but also in your life in heaven. It invites you to enjoy God as your Father now and reminds you that you will receive an inheritance from Him in the future. Now you enjoy the pleasure of knowing that God is your "Abba-Father." His love and commitment to you is unquestionable.

Look at one more place that Paul reminded us of what God offers. Titus 3:7 says, "having been justified by his grace we might become heirs having the hope of eternal life." God wants very much to give us everything we really need in this life. When we receive everything God desires to give us, we receive many rewards. Let's look at the rewards of knowing God as Daddy.

Reflection Questions:

1. Have you ever found yourself in the midst of negative circumstances but not doubting God?
2. How do you accept the spiritual reality that you "Ain't got there yet"?
3. How does God see you as better than you are?
4. How do you show your gratefulness to God for the relationship He offers you?
5. How is the cycle of intimacy with God like a funnel?
6. Can you identify with the steps on this journey?

Intimacy Exercise:

Think over your spiritual journey. Have you experienced the stages on this cycle? When?

Part 3

The Rewards of Knowing God as Daddy

11 The Path
of Divine Regression

But Jesus called the children to him and said, "Let the little children come to me, and do not hinder them, for the kingdom of God belongs to such as these. I tell you the truth, anyone who will not receive the kingdom of God like a little child will never enter it."

Luke 18:16–17

Greg did a stupid thing. He was lonely; he was mad; he was desperate; he wanted to get away from it all. He ignored the weatherman's warnings and headed out of town into the mountains of North Carolina, daring the threat of heavy downpours to thwart his plans. One thing he kept in the settlement of his recent divorce was the pop-up camper he had bought to try to bring the family together. Going on a camping trip alone seemed silly, but once the thought entered Greg's mind, nothing would sway his thinking. If the camper couldn't fix the mess of his marriage, he figured God owed him a weekend of restoration in it.

In spite of the blinding rain pounding on his windshield, Greg pressed forward. He figured the rain had to stop soon, and when it did, he would get what he came for—an escape from the chaos of his life. He planned to reach the campsite and then wait out the rain before setting up the pop-up. Less than fifteen minutes from his destination, he saw a car speeding down the mountain, honking. The driver stopped long enough to roll down his window and yell, "Mudslide! Turn around!"

"Turn around!" Greg told himself in a cynical tone. He was in the middle of his second maneuver, attempting to turn the truck and camper on the small mountainside road, when the mudslide hit. A tree branch crashed through the back window of his truck cab, and he was immediately buried in mud. Quickly he rolled down the driver's side window to allow some mud to escape. He found himself chest deep in a cold, cement-like trap, unable to free himself. Terror and loneliness crushed into his body and even deeper into his soul. No one was around. Foolishly, he hadn't told anyone where he was going. He wasn't sure if the man who had warned him had been able to escape and would bring help. The last place he remembered seeing his cell phone was on the floorboard of the cab. He had no way to reach it, and it couldn't possibly still work even if he could.

Just like a little child, in utter despair Greg prayed, "God, help . . . send help, please." He begged, "Please get me out of this. I can't do anything. I can't move, I can't breathe. . . . Please, please, please help." He was as helpless as a little child with no one to turn to but his Father.

After he prayed, Greg felt himself relax in the midst of the death trap that imprisoned him. For the first time in years, Greg had no plan, no ideas, and no determination to work things out on his own. An entire hour passed as he pondered the different ways God might rescue him, including by giving him miraculous strength to open the door and walk down the mountain. He even attempted to move his arms several times, but they wouldn't budge.

At the end of the hour, the answer to Greg's prayer drove up. It was a bulldozer equipped with four muscular men eager to find someone alive in the mess. At that moment Greg received what he drove up the mountain hoping to find. He realized that if God was willing to rescue him from the mess of the mudslide he got into by his own foolishness, then surely the mess of his life back home wasn't too much for God. Greg drove up that mountain with the arrogance of a grown man and little faith; he came down with the humility of a little child and faith that could move mudslides.

To progress in your spiritual journey, you've got to learn to pray in utter trust, like a child. When have you simply cried out, "Papa"? I was intrigued by a newspaper report about an earthquake that demolished the town of Celtiksuyu, Turkey, in 2003. Among the most damaged buildings was a school dormitory full of sleeping students. The report included this statement: "State television TRT showed a soldier carrying a boy from the school's wreckage and amid cheers from onlookers. The boy was shouting 'baba!' or father in Turkish."[1] Do you cry "Baba, Daddy, Papa" to your heavenly Father?

The utter trust between parent and child was shown when Jesus prayed in the Garden of Gethsemane, "Abba, Father . . . everything is possible for you. Take this cup from me. Yet not what I will but what you will" (Mark 14:36). The most important difference between the way Jesus prayed and so many other prayers that are shot off in anger is Jesus's confidence in the love and trust He received from His Daddy. Jesus knew how to be a child with His Father. When you start praying childlike prayers, you can know you are growing spiritually. Oswald Chambers describes this kind of spiritual maturity: "We grouse before God, we are apologetic or apathetic, but we ask very few things. Yet what a splendid audacity a childlike child has."[2] In 1 Peter 2:2 we are told to crave spiritual food like a newborn craves milk.

Evidently children have a lot to teach us about knowing God as Father and growing spiritually.

What Do Children Have to Teach Us?

Jesus said that you need to become like a little child if you are going to enter His kingdom. How do you know if you have received the kingdom as a little child? What did Jesus mean when He said that no one will enter the kingdom unless He enters as a little child (Luke 18:17)? It's worth considering.

What do you remember most fondly from your childhood? Think about your early years, when you could have been labeled a "little child." What was best about being a little child? Imagine yourself at five years old. What is on your five-year-old mind? Do you carry the weight of the world on your shoulders? Are you curious and eager and hopeful about life?

Unless your childhood included some extenuating circumstances (such as a severely dysfunctional family, crime, or a catastrophe happening to your family), remembering yourself as a little child should include a carefree innocence. At five, you are exploring a world you are just now feeling big enough to attempt to understand. You may get yourself in trouble from time to time and experience discipline and some disappointment. But for the most part, your world is free of heavy burdens. In your five-year-old mind all problems have solutions. Someone knows the answers to all your questions. You have faith that the answers are out there as you dare to ask why over and over again in complete sincerity. You believe in a world that is bigger than you can understand on your own. You believe that things can get better tomorrow. Even if your life is hard, you have hope that things could change.

Grasp Your Childishness

I don't think you will experience a genuine "Daddy" relationship with God until you embrace the humble freedom of
being like a little child before Him. I can feel your resistance.
You may want a deeper connection to God, but not if it means
that you regress into childhood. Surely this book is wrong. We
feel unnatural trying to see ourselves as little children. We are
self-sufficient beings. Growing into adulthood took a lot of
years. Now you have your freedom, your choices. You resist
going backward.

What you know is how to be an adult. You have mastered how
to be self-sufficient and not need others. You have become the
master of your universe. You've got your eyes on the fast track.
In fact, you may have picked up this book for that very reason.
Perhaps you thought it was time to master your relationship with
God and hoped this book would show you how.

What you don't know about is being a child. You've forgotten what that is like. You stopped being a child physically
long ago, and you haven't put much thought into being a child
lately. Well, it's time to think about it. In fact, Jesus asked the
disciples on more than one occasion to think about being a little
child (Matt. 11:25; 19:13–15; Mark 9:33–37; Luke 9:46–48;
18:15–17; John 3:1–9). In Matthew 19:13–15, Jesus was quick
to refute the disciples who were rebuking parents for bringing
little children to Him for a blessing. He told the disciples not
to hinder children from coming to Him because the kingdom
belongs to children.

When Jesus looked at little children, He saw in them a spiritual lesson that all those who truly seek to follow Him must learn.
He took time to touch the children and honor them because
they demonstrated something essential about His kingdom. You
cannot enter the kingdom unless you enter as a little child.

It Doesn't Feel Right

I remember the feeling of childishness I experienced during my first silent retreat. After we arrived, our leader told us not to spend long periods reading books and encouraged us to simply be with God. I had brought along my favorite books and planned to read them during the extended period without phones, television, or talking. This was the only thing I knew to do. I knew these special books had stimulated my relationship with God. I thought I would need them to be with God for an extended period of time.

I like to follow the rules, so I left my books lying in my suitcase. *Well, God,* I thought, *what do you want to do for the next thirty-eight hours? . . . Let's go canoeing.* I was quick to answer the questions I asked of God. God came along on my canoe trip and guided my mind to important messages He had for me as I traveled all around the lake. During the afternoon I took God on a walk, and we swung on a bench swing, watched the ants, and sat in the warm sunshine.

At the end of the day, I wrote in my journal what being with God was like. It was like I was a little girl convincing my "Daddy" to come along on my adventures. He was happy to oblige because He loved me. He cooperated and participated fully in my escapades, showing me lots of life-changing truths along the way. When I made this observation, I could see that it was a childish relationship. I felt like a spoiled little girl doing only what appealed to me. I never cared about His opinions or feelings. I felt I needed to grow up and become more mature spiritually. I felt a bit disappointed in myself and ashamed that I wasn't more mature. But that kind of thinking will cause us to miss out on the part of childhood that we must never outgrow. When I reject that part of me, I reject a special connection to God. I need to comprehend that childlike wonder should always be a part of my relationship to God. In some ways I never want to outgrow being a child spiritually.

Have you ever wished for the days when your dog was a puppy? If I could somehow make my dog a puppy again, I would love to visit those moments from time to time. Do your arms ever ache to hold your adult child like you used to when he was an infant? I just can't help believing that God wants to keep a little of that child part of our humanness in our relationship with Him because it is so special and unique. We need it, and He delights in it. God encourages me to stay in touch with my childhood to mature in my faith.

A Child Believes the Answers Are Too Big to Understand

You cannot have faith in Jesus Christ unless you have faith in what you cannot see or prove but wholeheartedly believe. This is the kind of faith that a little child expresses in her caretakers. Children accept that they cannot comprehend everything about their universe, yet they remain confident that they will some day.

Job demonstrated that childlike faith after all adult reasoning and logic failed him. You may be unfamiliar with the story of Job, but it is a must-read for every Christian. Job was passionate about God. God was passionate about Job. Job's passion for God had not been diverted by his great wealth and many earthly responsibilities. In fact, God's comment to Satan about Job was, "Have you considered my servant Job? There is no one on earth like him; he is blameless and upright, a man who fears God and shuns evil" (Job 1:8). Satan asked God to allow him to bring unbearable tragedy into Job's life to prove that Job would not trust God if he had to face difficult circumstances. God allowed Satan to plunder Job's wealth, belongings, and children, all in one day. I don't know of anyone who has ever faced the degree of loss that Job did that fateful day. Yet Job's childlike faith caused him to comment on his catastrophic losses: "'Naked I came from my mother's womb, and naked I will depart. The LORD gave and the LORD has taken away; may the name of the LORD be praised.' In all this, Job did not sin by charging God with wrongdoing" (Job 1:21–22).

In an effort to further discourage Job, Satan devised a second test and took away Job's health, sending painful boils to cover his body. Job remained faithful to God. Then Job was visited by four friends who sat in silence with him. After Job's counselors started talking, Job's childlike faith was replaced by adult logic and reason. This was the beginning of a decline in his spiritual condition. The counselors were convinced that Job had some secret or unknown sin that must be exposed. In Job's efforts to consider their comments, he lost touch with his sense of childlike faith and trust in God. He came to reason that God had somehow made a mistake.

At just the right time, God came to restore Job's childlike faith. God takes a surprising direction with Job. He doesn't sit down with him and go over the events of the recent past. He doesn't tell Job that Satan has been testing him in an effort to prove that humans were totally worthless and would never freely worship God if faced with suffering. God does not appeal to Job's adult ability to reason. Instead, God artfully ignites the flame of complete childlike faith in Job's soul once again.

He told Job that He is God and that He is bigger and wiser than Job and his adult thinking. He did this by asking Job a series of rhetorical questions like "Where were you when I created this vast universe?" "Do you know why the waves only go this far?" By the end of God's sixty-six questions Job replies with the heart of a child, "Surely I spoke of things I did not understand, things too wonderful for me to know" (Job 42:3).

Do you have the kind of faith that convinces you that God is too wonderful for you to fully understand? That is the faith of a little child. That is the faith of a mature saint. Are you one?

Children Say the Darndest Things

"Out of the mouths of babes" is an adage about childhood. We easily recognize the fact that sometimes children best reveal the futility of adult reasoning. Hans Christian Andersen featured this virtue in his tale "The Emperor's New Clothes." In the story, a couple of scoundrels came to town and talked the king into letting them make him the most magnificent clothing in the world. They told him it would be created from a modern fabric. In fact, the fabric was so special, the king was told, that simple-minded people could not even see it at all. It could only be seen by the noble and wise. What was the king to think when he saw his newly employed tailors sewing on fabric that was invisible to his own eyes? The members of the king's court reacted as if they could see the special fabric, and this just made the king more afraid to admit that he saw nothing. Once the "tailors" collected the money, they headed out of town. The king put on the invisible clothes and wore them in a parade through town. While all the people in town were commenting on the beauty of the fabric that wasn't there, a small child was the first to comment, "But he hasn't anything on."[3] And at once the truth was brought forth.

Children have a way of bringing us back to the basics. We often remember a story from when our son Ben was about five years old. He told his daddy, "I wish you wouldn't yell at me." Brian replied, "You know what? I have a sure way that I would never have to yell at you again. Just do everything I say, and I will never have to yell at you." In complete five-year-old innocence, Ben looked up at his daddy and said, "Okay, then you can call me 'Jesus.'" What a humbling conversation that was for my husband.

Sometimes we can get so caught up in the details of living that we miss out on the basics. You don't enter the kingdom because of anything you have done for God or any problem you have solved for God; you enter the kingdom because you have demonstrated the understanding of a child that you are a sinner and you are helpless without Christ to save you.

In Matthew 11:25–26 Jesus said, "I praise you, Father, Lord of heaven and earth, because you have hidden these things from the wise and learned, and revealed them to little children. Yes, Father, for this was your good pleasure." I am utterly amazed that the indescribable God of the universe takes delight in being understood by the littlest child. If you are going to progress in your knowledge of God, you must continue in the faith of a little child.

Children Listen to Their Parents

You don't realize how closely children are listening to you until you hear them say the words you shouldn't have said. This happened to me more times than I would like to think, but I remember the first time my daughter Rachel repeated one of my off-color words because my younger sister often reminds me of it. We were on a road trip, just the girls—my mom, two aunts, my younger sister, Rachel, and me. Rachel was around three. When the van door opened, her toy that was leaning against the door fell to the ground. Rachel looked at it and said, "Crap." My sister (herself childless at the time) was appalled at the words coming out of the mouth of such an innocent child. At that moment I first realized how much I must have said that word. I quickly cleaned up my language.

In parenting classes I often advise parents that children spend much more time studying us than we spend thinking of how to respond to them. They learn when we mean business. My own children used to ignore my instructions until I began them with the word "okay." They had deduced that when I started with "Okay . . ." it meant that I would follow through with consequences this time, so they'd better do what I said. Children are listening. Children are learning. Children are creating strategies for how to get what they want from their parents.

As a child before God, you will learn to love His Word. You will learn to treasure it, to store it in your heart. You won't tune Him out. You will see spiritual realities that others miss. You will listen to God and even hang on His words. And soon you will find yourself repeating the things He tells you. What comes out of your mouth will be similar to the things you read in the pages of Scripture. With a perfect parent to listen to, you will never be led astray by what you hear.

Children Don't Discriminate

Visit any preschool and you will discover that preschoolers don't choose their friends based on who is the richest, who is the smartest, or who has the best tricycle. Jesus felt that adults had a lot to learn from children on this point. Jesus used a little child as an object lesson after He found the disciples arguing about who was the greatest. After telling them that the way to be first is to be a servant, He pointed out a little child among them and told them that whoever welcomes little children in His name welcomes Him, and whoever welcomes Him welcomes God (Mark 9:33–37).

This is foreign to us as adults. In human relationships, if someone loves me, then he or she must love you less. That is not the case with God. God accepts us as sons and daughters. Everyone who has received redemption from their sins through Jesus Christ, God accepts in the same way He accepts His own Son Jesus Christ. No child of God has any reason to feel less loved than another.

Children Imitate Those They Admire

Another characteristic of children is their propensity for imitation. Studies show that when children watch something on television, they will frequently try to replicate the same behaviors in their play. My daughter was three years old when my husband and I were working on our dissertations. She was the only girl in her preschool who was working on her own dissertation as well. Even though she couldn't read or write, she was constantly making revisions on our discarded pages which she had stapled together.

Jesus invites us to be imitators of Him. My three-year-old daughter Rachel didn't let the fact that she couldn't read and write keep her from trying to prepare a dissertation. She was simply valuing what the people she loved valued. I shouldn't be distracted by the fact that Jesus was sinless and perfect but should attempt to imitate Him anyway.

The freedom to imitate what we don't fully understand is another characteristic of childhood that Jesus is looking for. Honestly, I can't imagine how God has the boldness to say some of the things He says. For example, in Galatians 5:16 He says that if I live by the Spirit, I won't sin. I don't know about you, but I've been a Christian for over three decades now and I have yet to cease from sin. The adult in me tells me I will never stop sinning, but childlike faith still believes that ceasing from sin is the goal I should strive for.

Children Never Get Enough

I remember countless times when my two children would fight to the last minute to stay awake so they wouldn't miss out on fun or excitement. I have several darling family photos of one of them falling asleep eating pizza or swinging at the park. Their bodies always gave out before their enthusiasm.

I was talking to my friend Carol the other day about being a child before God, and she relayed this story of when she felt that way. She was at a prayer conference with a group of people mostly unfamiliar to each other. The speaker at the conference invited individuals who had a specific need for prayer to come forward so she could pray for them. My friend prayed in her seat and could not think of a specific thing for which to ask for prayer. But something inside her wanted to take part in what she clearly saw God doing at the front of the building. She went forward anyway and told the leader that she just wanted to be a part of the prayer but there wasn't anything specific she had come to request. She loved taking part in this prayer and could feel God's presence.

The next day the leader offered the same invitation. Once again, Carol had no definite thought on her heart that needed prayer, even though the leader specifically asked those who had a particular request to come forward. She sat in her seat, kept back by her adult self chiding her for even wanting more prayer. Finally her childlike self won out, and once again she asked for prayer in spite of the fact that she didn't have a specific request.

She told me, "I was being like a child. A child can never get enough of a good thing. They always want more cookies." God invites you to be like a child before Him. Unlike with cookies, you can never get enough of Him.

Children Believe That Someone Bigger Understands What They Don't

I love the way Paul describes Abraham's childlike faith in Romans 4:18–21:

> Against all hope, Abraham in hope believed and so became the father of many nations, just as it had been said to him, "So shall your offspring be." Without weakening in his faith, he faced the fact that his body was as good as dead—since he was about a hundred years old—and that Sarah's womb was also dead. Yet he did not waver through unbelief regarding the promise of God, but was strengthened in his faith and gave glory to God, being fully persuaded that God had power to do what he had promised.

Even at one hundred years old, Abraham reveals childlike faith to us. Can you imagine believing that God was going to make you a biological father at one hundred years old? And even more unfathomable, that the baby would come from the womb of your ninety-year-old wife? That is childlike faith.

I love the old candy commercial where a little girl is sitting with her daddy watching a sunrise. Just as the sun breaks through the dawn and rises to cover the earth, she looks to her dad and whispers, "Do it again, Daddy." That's childlike faith—believing in wonder that your Father can do anything!

Children Depend on Others to Solve Their Problems

Children have problems that they cannot manage on their own. They don't think they have to have all the answers. They have learned to depend on people who do have the answers to their problems.

Children ask questions because they aren't afraid of the answers. I love to be around five-year-olds. They ask the best questions. I kept a journal about my kids, including some of the questions they asked, like: "Can God swim?" "Why did God make mosquitoes?" "Why has God never sinned?" You will have lots of questions for God. Many of His answers are beyond our human comprehension. For example, why will so few of earth's inhabitants come to a saving knowledge of Jesus? Why is Satan permitted to wreak such havoc in this world? Those are tough ones. If you trust God as your Dad, you will ask. Only He can answer in a way that brings peace beyond understanding (Phil. 4:7).

Becoming a Child Is a Spiritual Miracle

Nicodemus was a wise man. He was a religious man. He was a careful man. Unlike the majority of the religious leaders (he was part of the Jewish ruling council), he did not think that Jesus could do the miracles He did except through the power of God. Still, Nicodemus was thorough. Even though Jesus seemed to be sent from God, most of Nicodemus's friends were against Jesus. So Nicodemus came to Jesus at night. Jesus explained to Nicodemus that he could not recognize the things of God unless he was born again. Nicodemus thought this was ludicrous. The laws of nature will not permit an adult to reenter his mother's womb to be born again. Jesus told him that the birth was not a physical birth but a spiritual birth (see John 3:1–6).

Everyone who comes to God through faith in Jesus Christ is born again. It's difficult to explain to those who've never experienced it. Being born again is a miracle that defies explanation. When you are born again spiritually, you acquire many of the positive earmarks of a child. These characteristics increase as you mature.

Visualize Yourself as a Child with Your Abba Father

Imagine yourself as one of the children waiting to be blessed by Jesus. Envision your parents bringing you to Jesus and the disciples telling you and your parents to go away and not bother the teacher. Feel the disappointment and the shame. See yourself turning away to leave, feeling hurt and rejected. Then listen to Jesus as He rebukes the ones who just rebuked you. His tone is indignant, much more forceful than the disciples had been with you.

In utter revolt against the way you have been treated, Jesus calls out to you and your parents to return. He picks you up and holds you in His arms, and then He uses you as a lesson for the disciples. He tells them that they must come to Him like you have, as a little child. He says that the kingdom of God belongs to those who come to Jesus in the manner you have come.

You may not understand everything that is going on that day, but you are amazed by the love that is flowing from Jesus to you. You know that you like being in the arms of Jesus and hearing His words of blessing. His hands rest on your head as He prays for you. You know you will never forget this experience.

When was the last time you came to Jesus and God as a little child? Why not put down this book right now and read Mark 10:13–16? Respond to Jesus's invitation to come to Him as a little child. Close your eyes and let yourself be in His presence as a child. Feel the tenderness of His Daddy love for you. Write about your experience in your prayer journal. How do you hold on to this truth every day? How do you remember whose child you are?

Reflection Questions:

1. What characteristics of childhood is Jesus looking for in mature Christians?
2. Why is it important to come to God as a little child?
3. Why doesn't it feel right to come to Jesus as a little child?
4. How have you shown the faith of a little child?
5. What lessons do little children teach us?
6. What childlike characteristics do you possess?

Intimacy Exercise:

Write a letter to your Daddy-God. Use your opposite writing hand if it will help you connect better to the child you are before God.

12 Knowing Whose Child You Are

The devil said to him, "If you are the Son of God, tell this stone to become bread."

Luke 4:3

My sister-in-law and I are both named Debbie, although we spell it differently. I received a phone call from one of my sister-in-law's friends while she was visiting my home in Texas. Her friend asked, "Can I speak to Debbie Bowles?" My automatic response was, "Yes, this is she." The friend said, "No, I need to speak to Debbie *Bowles*." Once again I assured her that she was indeed speaking to Debi Bowles. She then said, "You are not Debbie Bowles; you are Debi Newman. I need to speak with Debbie Bowles." Instantly I was snapped back into reality and finally conceded that I was not Debbie Bowles.

The reason for the confusion was that I had been Debi Bowles for twenty-three years. When the caller asked for that person, my automatic response was "This is she." I claimed Debi Bowles as my identity despite the fact that I was no longer identified by that name. I was now married and had taken a new name, Debi Newman. This is the way I am identified to friends and family. When I forgot my new identity, I confused myself and everyone else.

I was born into this world as the daughter of Bob and Norma Bowles. When I was seven years old I claimed my new identity as God's daughter. Sometimes I forget who I am. I don't live in the freedom of my true spiritual identity. Instead I try to live up to what others expect of me. I work on being known for my achievements and accomplishments rather than as God's daughter. Our lifelong spiritual journey involves accepting our new identity so fully that when someone calls us on the phone and asks to speak to God's daughter (or son), we immediately answer, "That's me!"

Even more important is accepting our new identity so that when the enemy calls to address you by your past sins, you do not let him make you believe you are worthless any longer. Henri Nouwen writes, "Self-rejection is the greatest enemy of the spiritual life because it contradicts the sacred voice that calls us the 'Beloved.' Being the beloved expresses the core truth of our existence."[1] Knowing God as Father naturally leads to knowing yourself as a child of God. Every child of God is free of condemnation. My favorite Scripture is Romans 8:1, "Therefore, there is now no condemnation for those who are in Christ Jesus." Self-condemnation is the enemy of your spiritual life; it is the enemy of your soul.

I read one of those sappy emails that brought home an important point about the journey of knowing who you really are. The email story was about a nurse who was treating an elderly man for a medical condition. The man told her that he was in a hurry and had an important appointment at 9:00 a.m. that he couldn't miss. The nurse felt sympathy for the man and personally worked with him to get him out of the office and to his appointment on time. While she was treating him she asked what the appointment was for. He informed her that he was to eat breakfast with his wife in the nursing home. She had Alzheimer's. The nurse commented, "But she doesn't even know who you are. Why is it important that you keep this appointment?" The man informed her, "She may not know who I am, but I know who she is." Though we often walk around with spiritual Alzheimer's, not knowing who we really are, God knows who we are. He never stops showing up to remind us in simple ways. Unlike Alzheimer's disease, spiritual Alzheimer's has a cure. You can learn to grasp your true identity.

Grasping Your True Identity

First John 3:1 says, "How great is the love the Father has lavished on us, that we should be called children of God! And that is what we are!" Do you know exactly who you are? Luke 3:22 tells us that when Jesus was baptized, He heard a voice out of heaven saying, "You are my Son, whom I love; with you I am well pleased." Immediately after this spiritual experience, Jesus was led by the Spirit into the wilderness to be tempted. How did Satan tempt Him? Satan tempted Him to prove that He was the Son of God. He challenged Him, "If you are the Son of God, then . . ." Jesus knew He was the Son of God. That is how He passed Satan's tests. When you really know that you are the son or daughter of God, you will find yourself victorious over the clutch of the enemy.

You too will be tempted. When someone else gets the job you wanted, you will be tempted to think that God does not care for you. When you blow it again and yell at your wife, judge your neighbor, watch that television show, you will be tempted to think that God couldn't possibly still care for you now. You will be tempted to doubt your worth to God when others reject or show little interest in you. Henri Nouwen wrote, "The great spiritual task facing me is to so fully trust that I belong to God that I can be free in the world—free to speak even when my words are not received; free to act even when my actions are criticized, ridiculed, or considered useless; free also to receive love from people and to be grateful for all the signs of God's presence in the world. I am convinced that I will truly be able to love the world when I fully believe that I am loved far beyond its boundaries."[2]

Do you know that exactly who you are is God's child? You are loved beyond the boundaries of this universe. Luke's Gospel gives Jesus's genealogy all the way back to Adam, who is called the son of God. You need to know your spiritual genealogy. All of our genealogies take us back to the same place. We are all the son of Adam, the son of God. We are God's children. This is our true identity.

I know these truths; I've been transformed by them. Still, I find myself pushed down by the condemnation in my world. Really loving God as Father should leave you with a sense of knowing yourself as His child. We fail to live up to this freeing identity in some common ways. How will you see God when you know you are His child?

You Are God's Child, Not God!

Recently I spoke to a friend who was struggling with her body image. She felt like a complete fool for being at this place again. Several years before, God had set her free from the prison of body hate that trapped her mind because of past sexual abuse by her father. After she was set free of this body hate, which had included twenty years of bulimia, she had become a popular Bible teacher. People turned to her for spiritual guidance and direction. She encouraged young girls and women who were struggling with eating disorders. She had given testimony after testimony about the way God set her free from bulimia. She encouraged women not to listen to Satan's lies about their bodies.

She thought she would never reject her body again. That's exactly when it happened. When the thoughts of her normal weight gain because of age kept creeping in, she told herself she was past all that. She wouldn't even admit to herself that she was unsatisfied with the ten extra pounds. Deep down she may have been afraid that if she even thought about it, she would become bulimic again. Instead she completely condemned herself for even having a negative thought about her body. She thought of all the people she would let down. She had to keep her chin up or no one would believe they could really get over an eating disorder. She felt like all the hopes of every person who had ever heard her testimony were on her shoulders. As thoughts like these increased, the number of negative thoughts about her body grew more intense. Feeling the need to keep these thoughts secret was the perfect breeding ground for them to grow to the point that they consumed her life. Shame begets shame, and she was in a rapid downward spiral.

When she finally talked to me about it, I told her that her need to readjust to her changing body was natural. It didn't mean that she was going backward and that she had lied to hundreds of people. In fact, she needed to continue doing the things she had done before to set her free from bulimia in the first place.

We lose touch with our true identity when we mistakenly take the credit for the victories in our lives. When we truly do things in Christ, we aren't the ones doing the work.

I was reminded of this spiritual reality while on a mother-son retreat. It included many activities for mothers and sons to enjoy. One of the "fun" opportunities that we had was the "Screamer." My son was an old pro at the Screamer since the retreat center was the same place he went for summer camp. It was my first time.

When I explain what the Screamer is, you will agree that it is well named. The Screamer is an activity where you climb up a thirty-foot pole, stand on a miniscule platform, get tied to a rope, and then fall forward into the air. I should mention that several safety features are in place to insure that although you may have a nervous breakdown carrying out this task, your body will be kept from harm.

When my turn came, I started my ascent up the tall pole. I climbed with the help of spikes sticking out of the pole that allowed me to lift my body higher and higher. The realization that I was not in this on my own hit me when I came to the end of the spikes. I was still about two feet away from that tiny platform I was supposed to stand on. "How do I get up there?" I called to the young man below holding the belay rope. "I'll help you," he said. I'm not sure exactly what I did at this point—I think I grabbed onto something and tried to lift myself—but whatever I did, the rest was done for me. I made it. I was secure aboard my tiny plank of safety.

So far, so good. I enjoyed pleasant conversation with the nice gentleman whose job it was to make sure that participants were safely hooked into the device that would hold them in their free-falling descent from the thirty-foot pole. He shared some of his experiences encouraging people to let go and complete their jump. He hooked me in and told me to sit down on the platform.

After this he spoke the words that I had heard him speak several times while I waited in line: "Grab the rope and fall forward off the platform." I knew these words well. I knew they were coming. This was the whole reason I had climbed up there in the first place. My goal was to free-fall from a pole thirty feet in the air. I wanted to tell everyone, especially my son, that I did it.

But that purpose seemed a stupid one when I sat in position ready to take off. I tried. I leaned forward. (My hands are even sweating as I replay this story in my mind.) I just couldn't do it. I asked for help. I said, "You're going to have to push me. On the count of three: one, two, three!" He pushed, I screamed, I laughed, I swung. It was a blast. I got down. Now I could tell Ben I did it. But that wasn't really true. I did it, but only with a lot of help. I didn't do it alone. I couldn't even climb onto the platform without help. I couldn't make myself fall forward without a push. I couldn't have stayed calm without prayer.

Weakness really isn't all that bad when it brings you face to face with the strength you really need. The wonderful truth about being God's child is that God can accomplish through you what you could never accomplish in your own strength. Recognizing that you are God's child, not God, is both freeing and empowering.

Every Child Is His Favorite

It's part of our sin nature to want to be the best. We learned from a friend who had one daughter and one son that you can always say you have a favorite daughter and a favorite son when you only have two children, a girl and a boy. We thought we had found a great way to balance sibling rivalry. It didn't work. Children can see right through that; being the favorite child doesn't mean anything to them if they are the only child.

God doesn't have favorites! God shows a lot of favor toward mankind in general, and He is able to abundantly bless those who devote themselves to Him, but He doesn't have favorites. We have a hard time reconciling this in our minds. Our human relationships are steeped with rewards for those who have more money, more talents, or more intelligence. The pretty one, the smart one—that's who you want to be. We have difficulty conceiving of a God who made us each unique and, although He loves us equally, disperses earthly favors to differing degrees for His own reasons, which may not be easily distinguished by the human eye.

I talked to a young man who was livid with God for blessing his older brother with a six-figure income even though he wasn't following God. I asked him, "What makes you so sure that having a six-figure income is a blessing from God?" When Jesus visited our universe, God chose for Jesus to stay with a couple who couldn't even afford the best sacrifice to celebrate His birth. When Mary and Joseph brought Jesus to the temple they brought a dove sacrifice indicating they could not afford a lamb. For Jesus, even the most extravagant luxury on the Earth would be slumming it. He didn't live in luxury by the standards of that time. Was this man's brother truly blessed by God if his six-figure income was enticing him to spend less time thinking about God? The truth is, you can't determine God's favorites by bank accounts.

Jesus doesn't want us to compare ourselves to each other anyway (2 Cor. 10:12). This favorite syndrome showed its ugly head during one of Peter's last conversations with Jesus on earth. Jesus singled him out to talk to him about his future ministry and to restore him after his embarrassing denial. Jesus warned Peter about the way he would die. Upon hearing this news about himself, Peter's next question was about John. How would he die? Jesus told Peter, "If I want him to remain alive until I return, what is that to you? You must follow me" (John 21:22).

Jesus didn't love Mary more than Martha when He told Martha that Mary had chosen what was better (Luke 10:38–42). Mary was naturally a more contemplative person and Martha a woman of action. He didn't tell Martha to worship Him in the same way Mary did. Nor did He value the way one sister worshiped over the other. He was pointing out to Martha that she was worried and distracted in His presence. John 12:2 shows Jesus's approval of Martha as the Scripture simply tells us, "Martha served." Martha worshiped Jesus by her service. Mary worshiped Jesus with her extravagant expression of pouring costly perfume over His head (John 12:3). Both were beautiful acts of devotion to Jesus.

His Voice Is Distinct

If you put me in a room, filled it up with hundreds of men, and asked my dad to be there and clear his throat, I could find him in a minute. He has a distinct way of clearing his throat that sets him apart. I know my dad by the way he clears his throat.

Children are quite adept at knowing their parents' voices. I love to tell Ben the story of his birth. The room had about five people in it, all hovering over his tiny body, talking to him and each other. The room was full of bright lights and noise, but when they held Ben up for me to see him and I called his name, he looked right at me. Everyone smiled and said, "He knows that is his mother." At only minutes old, he could distinguish my voice from all the other foreign sounds his ears were taking in.

For many years in my Christian life I thought I was listening to the voice of God. Later I discovered that the voice that badgered me about and condemned me for my sins was not His voice at all. When God convicts me of sin, He calls me by name. At the very beginning of sin, God came to the garden and called Adam by name. God is not the voice of condemnation. The voice that accuses me of sin comes from Satan (Rev. 12:10). The voice that lovingly confronts me with my sin is God's (Rom. 2:4).

God speaks most clearly in His Word. When I feel God telling me something in my mind or spirit, I need to make sure that it doesn't contradict His Word. I encourage you to keep a journal of thoughts you think God is speaking to you. Talk about these thoughts with a mature Christian who can give you feedback regarding what you are hearing. Look for confirmation in God's Word. Ask God to assure you about what you think He is saying.

You Need Sober Judgment

Paul instructs us to have sober judgment. In Romans 12:3 he writes, "For by the grace given me I say to every one of you: Do not think of yourself more highly than you ought, but rather think of yourself with sober judgment, in accordance with the measure of faith God has given you." Our sin nature leads us to think more highly of ourselves than we should. This is something we all struggle with. Actually, if you are thinking lowly of yourself, your standards for yourself may be too high. God doesn't want us to think lowly of ourselves or too highly of ourselves. He tells us to have sober judgment.

Self-rejection has become such a normal part of our lives that we find receiving what God offers hard. When we reject ourselves, we are rejecting God. Sober judgment contradicts self-rejection. Sober judgment is finding your acceptance in God. It is faith in God's evaluation of you.

As God's child you have every reason to think of yourself in a sober way, according to the faith that God has given you. If you are doing outstanding things for God—even more than the other Christians you know—God says, "You are not better than the others; I gave you a greater measure of faith. It's actually Me who is using you, not you who are so great!" We've got to get that straight. Just because God decides to use a certain person like Billy Graham in a worldwide way and Billy Jones in a smaller realm of influence doesn't mean that God likes Billy Graham more than Billy Jones. What matters to God is that you are living up to the measure of faith that He has given you.

How Are You Supposed to Think of Yourself?

Jesus's core identity was thinking of Himself as the Son of God. During Jesus's mock trial, He made very few statements. In fact, He was completely silent before Herod, and Pilate was stunned at His unwillingness to defend Himself when questioned. The one thing that caused Him to break His silence when He was on trial before the Sanhedrin was when He was asked if He was the Son of God. He answered assertively in the positive, even though this admission further enraged the high priest. Jesus knew whose Son He was, and this truth became an anchor for His soul. If someone called your home and asked to speak to God's son (or daughter), what would your response be?

Reflection Questions:

1. What kind of love does God have for us that causes Him to claim us as His sons and daughters?
2. How do you remember that you are His daughter or son?
3. How did Jesus face the rejection and difficulty of His life as God's Son?
4. What are some of the common pitfalls we stumble over as we try to see ourselves as God's sons and daughters?
5. How do you hear God's voice?
6. What does it mean to have sober judgment regarding yourself?

Intimacy Exercise:

Make a list of identities you have claimed in the past or names you have been called. Cross them all out and write beside each one "Child of God" as your new identity.

13 The Heart of a Father

As the Father has loved me, so have I loved you. Now remain in my love.

John 15:9

I don't think I know another man as proud to become a father as my husband. Although he was more reluctant than I was to start down the path of parenthood, once he knew he would be a father, his attitude totally changed. He set out to videotape every milestone of our children's lives. We didn't even have a VCR in 1987 when we were pregnant with our first child, but he bought a video camera before we had a crib. We only have two children, but we have more than fifty hours of video.

Brian learned everything he could about being a father. In fact, he was reading a book about raising a son while I was in labor with our second born, our only son. Brian loves being a father and became quite adept at taking care of our children. He regularly took them on outings when I worked on Saturdays, and he has never missed a major event in their lives.

Simply getting a woman pregnant does not make a man a true father. Many men do a wonderful job at fathering though they have no blood relationship to the children they parent. A real father is someone who cares for, sacrifices for, and loves his children. By all these standards Brian is one of the best fathers I know. But being a good father didn't come naturally for him. He had to work at it. He was willing to listen to me when I told him how the babies liked to be held (after I had spent the day with them and discovered their likes and dislikes). He also had to be willing to disagree with me and swing them in the air to their delight and my dismay. Work, sacrifice, and willingness to enter into new territory were required for Brian to develop into the father he became.

The story of the prodigal son has three main characters: the prodigal son, the elder brother, and the father. In Henri Nouwen's book *The Return of the Prodigal Son*, he encourages readers to recognize the ways that they are like the prodigal son who left home and traveled to a distant land. He also reveals the ways readers are like the elder brother, not truly being home though they never left. Ultimately, he says, we all need to become like the father, giving away the gifts we have received.

Are you ready to love others the way you have learned to love God? I feel inspired by the line from the Broadway musical *Les Miserables*, "To love another person is to see the face of God." Nothing makes your heavenly Father more pleased than to see His children acting just like Him. You will never be closer to Him than when you love like Him.

How You Become like Your Father

I still remember the words of my obstetrician right after Ben was born. He commented on what a big baby Ben was (nine pounds, two-and-a-half ounces) and how healthy he looked. Then he said, "I've never seen a newborn look more like his father." It was true. People used to say that Rachel looked just like her father until Ben was born. Ben and Brian are virtual look-alikes. When I compared Brian's newborn pictures to Ben's, they could have been the same baby.

Personality-wise, they are both witty and funny, sometimes too much so for their own good (especially when it comes to school settings). Ben has many natural characteristics that are similar to his father. You could say that Ben is made in Brian's image.

They are still two different people, though. If Ben wants to be like his father, he will need to make choices to follow Brian's example. Even though he bears a striking resemblance to his father, he needs to do some things to become like him. He may have some natural characteristics that are similar, but a lot of who his father is and what his father has done and can do is different from Ben. If Ben's goal was to be just like his father, he would need to work to become that way. He would need to study his father and learn how Brian became the man he is today.

You bear the image of God (Gen. 1:26). That is not enough to make you like your Father. If you want to be like Him, you will need determination. It will include a total transformation of your soul. You will go from a self-centered prodigal son and a self-righteous elder brother to an others-centered father. This change is not natural; it is supernatural. Henri Nouwen makes this observation about the father in the parable of the prodigal son: "But the father of the prodigal son is not concerned about himself. His long-suffering life has emptied him of his desires to keep in control of things. His children are his only concern, to them he wants to give himself completely, and of them he wants to pour out all of himself."[1] This is what you have to look forward to if you desire to move further in the process and be truly transformed by the love of the Father to the degree that you become like Him.

You Will Love Those Your Father Loves

Once you really learn to love God as your Father, you will desire to love those your Father loves. God loves some pretty shady people. He even loves the likes of you. Loving God as your Father fills you with so much love that you begin to have different values. From the day you were born, you've been trying to get your own needs met. When you truly settle into the love of a Father, you will sincerely desire to reach out to others.

Jeremy was so moved by his unexpected experience that he had to share it with everyone when he returned from visiting an orphanage in Guatemala. He wrote: "I am amazed as I write this a week later that one girl could impact my life in such a way as Ana did. I came on this trip to bring God's love to orphans, to bring shoes, clothes, and medicine. I didn't realize what would be given to me. I truly received more than I gave."

Jeremy met Ana when he and his team were invited into the dormitories to put the children to bed after they had ministered to them through Vacation Bible School all day. He had been around boys a lot in his life, but somehow he was drawn to the girls' side. Several girls lived in one room filled from wall to wall with bunk beds and a locker for their personal belongings. The girls gathered around the adults, grabbing their hands and leading them to their little space in the world to show them their treasures—the shoes, candy, and toys that the mission team had brought.

One particular girl, Ana, pulled Jeremy into her space and into her heart. She had received a comb from the team. Jeremy said,

I'm not a father, so I don't have the instincts of a parent, but I knew the thing to do was to brush her hair. After I stopped brushing her hair, I gave her back the comb, and she turned to face me and started to brush my hair. I stopped her, not knowing if that was the right thing to do, and she looked at me as if to say: "What's wrong? Why did you pull away from me?" I felt terrible. I hugged her, and we began to rock back and forth. She sat in my lap, and I looked into her eyes, eyes so deep, so full of love.

People were singing in the room, and Jeremy attempted to sing "Jesus Loves Me" in Spanish. He made lots of mistakes, and each time Ana looked up and smiled. Several girls gathered around him as he sang. The director said it was time for bed, and the team helped the girls settle in their beds; they prayed and kissed them goodnight. Ana climbed into her top bunk and Jeremy placed her doll on her pillow. Their eyes met again and Jeremy reached through the slats on the bed and ran his fingers through her hair, stroking her head. Instinctively, he started singing "Jesus Loves Me" in Spanish again, and as her eyelids slowly began to close, his own filled with tears. Ana was asleep, but Jeremy noticed other girls who were still awake, still in need of a father's touch. He left Ana and moved from bed to bed, continuing to sing until each girl was asleep.

Jeremy said, "Who would have thought that a comb from a little girl would be a vessel of change?" Jeremy was the arms and voice of the heavenly Father for these much-loved girls in an orphanage in Guatemala. God has not forgotten them.

You Are Called to Be like the Father

First Peter 1:16 amazes me—God says, "Be holy, because I am holy." God actually invites me to be like Him. I must confess, sometimes I can be condescending. I might think that someone I am talking to can't understand a spiritual truth at their stage of their journey because it took me so long to learn myself. I've been proven wrong on more than one occasion. In the same way, God expects so much more of me than I think I'm capable of. God says, "Be holy, because I am holy."

Notice the reason we are to be holy. It is not because we are so great and capable of holiness. It is not because we want to show the world that we are better than everyone else. The one and only reason that we should pursue holiness is because God our Father is holy. Because He is holy, I should want to be holy too. The only way I could become holy was through the holiness of His Son. My holiness is all about God and deep relationship with Him.

God offers us all these exciting truths about how much He loves us, how He will never forsake us, how He wants to re-ward us, and how much He wants to hold us close because He knows that we will be changed by this intimate relationship. Our change is not a condition of the intimate relationship but an outcome of it.

If you do not find yourself changing into the likeness of your Father, I think you should consider what is really happening in your spiritual life. When I do physical exercise, I notice changes. In fact, the changes are what motivate me to keep exercising even though I hate to exercise. I first started exercising in my thirties because of my high cholesterol. Through exercise I was able to lower my cholesterol. I kept exercising. In my forties I gained weight. I still exercised, but I also needed to change the way I ate. My exercise alone was not keeping me healthy. I read a magazine article about people who exercise but don't lose weight or see the changes in their bodies that they expect. This article suggested that such a person needed to change his or her aerobic program. I had been exercising the same way for over ten years. I did thirty minutes of cardio on our home machine and a little bit of resistance training. After I read the article, I did what the writer suggested and added variety to my exercise program, and it worked. I saw the changes again. Likewise, you should see evidence that you are going through this spiritual cycle. You should be different.

I want to comfort you with the thought that the changes will be similar to those from exercise. They are subtle if you look day to day. You usually only see them when you mark your progress over months and years. God does not get discouraged with our slow progress. He just wants us making progress. We are usually the ones who think it should happen faster than it does. If you are moving deeper in your relationship with God, you should notice yourself becoming more willing to forgive, less selfish in traffic, or less defensive with others. You should notice that you are becoming more like your Father.

Jesus Was the Exact Representation of His Father

When the disciples asked to see the Father, Jesus told them that if they had seen Him, they had seen the Father (John 14:9). Jesus wants us to know that He was the exact representation of the Father. He declared, "Don't you believe that I am in the Father, and that the Father is in me? The words I say to you are not just my own. Rather, it is the Father, living in me, who is doing his work. Believe me when I say that I am in the Father and the Father is in me; or at least believe on the evidence of the miracles themselves" (John 14:10–11). Absolutely everything we witness about Jesus through the texts telling us about Him is the work of the Father.

Our deepening intimacy with God does not make us into the Father, but it incites us to want to be like the Father. The Father knows we will want to be like Him—for the right reasons, not for the wrong ones like Eve (Gen. 3:5–6) and Satan (Ezek. 28). God gives us help to be like Him through giving us the gift of the Holy Spirit living in our hearts. The Holy Spirit aids us as we draw close to God and really know Him as Father and also helps us be like Him as Father.

How You Live like the Father

As you come to know God as your Father, living like the Father becomes the deepest yearning of your soul. You want to stop being so petty. You want to have an eternal perspective and not sweat the small stuff. You want to be holy. Something in God's command to be holy because He is holy inspires you to want to do it. The truth is that being like the Father is not about power and victory. It doesn't always look like success. Henri Nouwen describes the way living like the Father will look in our lives: "There is a dreadful emptiness in this spiritual fatherhood. No power, no success, no popularity, no easy satisfaction. But that same dreadful emptiness is also the place of true freedom. It is the place where there is 'nothing left to lose,' where love has no strings attached, and where real spiritual strength is found."[2] And, he said, "Jesus is the freest human being who ever lived because he was the most connected to God."[3]

Bernard of Clairvaux, a twelfth-century French pastor, defined spiritual growth in these four stages:

1. Love of self for self's sake
2. Love of God for self's sake
3. Love of God for God's sake
4. Love of self for God's sake[4]

We are natural-born self-lovers. The process of responding to God's love matures us to the place of loving ourselves for God's sake. When we do, we will come to really love God as Father.

Do you have enemies? Are you good to them? Do you lend to them without expecting to get anything back? If you do these things, then you are like your Father. Luke 6:35–36 says, "But love your enemies, do good to them, and lend to them without expecting to get anything back. Then your reward will be great, and you will be sons of the Most High, because he is kind to the ungrateful and wicked. Be merciful, just as your Father is merciful."

Look around the world. How do you see God being kind to the ungrateful and wicked? God says He will reward us when He sees us being merciful to others. This is exactly what the father of the prodigal son demonstrated to both his sons.

Before you go down the trail of thought, *Surely God doesn't expect me to be as kind, merciful, and forgiving as the Father*, read Jesus's words in Luke 6:40: "A student is not above his teacher, but everyone who is fully trained will be like his teacher."

My prayer for you is that when you follow this funnel-shaped cycle to its end, you will find yourself happy and safe in the arms of your Father. Os Guinness puts it this way: "After a lifetime of journeying, we are arriving home. After all the years of hearing only the voice, we are about to see the face and feel the arms. The Caller is our Father and the Last Call is the call home."[5]

Nothing but good can come out of your quest to really love God as Father. You were created to be His child. You were made brother and sister with Jesus through His sacrifice on the cross and have been empowered by the Holy Spirit to live in the holiness that you are meant for. Continue along your journey. Enjoy the process of getting to know God so intimately that you can call him "Abba"—Papa-Daddy, your most loving Father.

A Final Thought

Really loving God as your Father is one of the most satisfying experiences on earth. What an honor it is to be the child of God. What a privilege to have a perfect Father to love.

Really loving God as your Father can be disappointing. Once you see God as your Father and see yourself as an honored child you think, "How can I ever sin again?" God is a perfect Father, but you and I are not perfect yet.

Cultivating your Father-child relationship will require much patience with yourself. Don't doubt God because you are not able to live up to all He offers you. Just keep on holding on to your Father's hand. Never let go of the hope that there is nothing you could do to stop your Father from loving you.

In this book I have shared the cycle I have experienced which has deepened my relationship with God. For me, intimacy with God has been not a destination but a journey. I find myself sailing along spiritually, thinking I'm a pretty good person, enjoying how close I feel to God, when suddenly I face a whole new level of brokenness that invites me to move deeper into relationship with God. That's when I return to the cycle we've gone over.

Cycle

When I'm broken before God, I'm not weak. It feels right; He is gentle and kind. I don't cringe so much anymore when I face brokenness. Perhaps I experience it this way because I know what is coming, the next step on the cycle: comfort. God's comfort is like nothing else. It is like a sacred embrace.

Once God has my attention on the amazing relationship He offers me, I'm ready to trust Him to guide my life. I receive His guidance and I know what I ought to do, but still I need help. He gives me the strength to follow His will for my life. Feeling the power of God at work in me, knowing He guides me, and being assured of His comfort in spite of my brokenness leads to the loving, emotional closeness that my soul groans for. The experience of emotional closeness is the fifth point of the cycle of intimacy with God. The strength of our relationship is often tested. God doesn't test me to hurt me but to make my faith strong.

Over the years I have observed that my journey to the heart of God follows these familiar and freeing steps. They help me grow deeper, closer, and more confident in the love of a Father I can call "Daddy." By confidently following this path, I hope to hear my Father say about me, "This is my daughter, in whom I am well pleased."

The cycle brings inspiration to me and draws me close to God. I find so many benefits in knowing I'm a child of God, and my prayer is that you are well on your way to knowing and loving God in this way.

Reflection Questions:

1. How are you like the older son?
2. How are you like the prodigal son?
3. How are you like the father?
4. Why does God want us to be holy?
5. What makes God a proud Papa when he looks at your life?
6. What stage are you on in the cycle of knowing God as Father? How often have you traveled the cycle?

Identity Exercise:

Make a list of ways you can be like the Father. Begin to fulfill these ideas in your daily life.

Notes

Chapter 1 You Can Call God "Daddy"

1. Lindley Baldwin, *Samuel Morris* (Minneapolis: Bethany, 1942), 16.
2. Henri Nouwen, *Bread for the Journey* (New York: HarperCollins, 1997), June 11.
3. Brennan Manning, *Abba's Child—The Cry of the Heart for Intimate Belonging* (Colorado Springs: NavPress, 1994), 64.

Chapter 2 The Orphaned Soul

1. *The Complete Works of E. M. Bounds on Prayer* (Grand Rapids: Baker, 1990), 10.
2. Terry W. Glasprey, *Pathway to the Heart of God* (Eugene, OR: Harvest House, 1998), 16.
3. Bob Woodward, interview by Mike Wallace, *60 Minutes*, CBS, April 18, 2004.

Chapter 3 You Are a Child of the King

1. *Les Miserables*, DVD, directed by Bille August (Columbia/Tristar Home Entertainment, 1998).
2. Philip Yancey, *The Bible Jesus Read* (Grand Rapids: Zondervan, 1999), 33.
3. Creath Davis, quoted by Verdell Davis Krisher, from Silent Retreat 2001.

Chapter 4 The Basics of Brokenness

1. Max Lucado, *A Gentle Thunder* (Dallas: Word, 1995), 121.
2. Louis Evely, *That Man Is You* (New York: Paulist Press, 1967), 72.

Chapter 5 The Healing Power of Comfort

1. Mrs. Charles E. Cowman, *Streams in the Desert* (Grand Rapids: Zondervan, 1965), 202.

2. Henri Nouwen, *The Inner Voice of Love* (New York: Doubleday, 1996), 26–27.

3. Ibid.

4. Ibid.

5. Oswald Chambers, *My Utmost for His Highest* (Uhrichville, OH: Barbour, 1963), June 25.

Chapter 6 Responding to the Light

1. Robert J. Morgan, *On This Day* (Nashville: Thomas Nelson, 1997), January 15.

2. R. C. Trench, quoted in Glasprey, *Pathway to the Heart of God*, 35.

Chapter 7 The Power of Relationship

1. Dana Christmas, "A Flash of White," *Angels of Earth*, January/February 2002, 33–37.

2. Chambers, *My Utmost for His Highest*, December 3.

Chapter 9 The Discipline of Intimacy

1. Dr. James A. Danoff-Burg, "The Determiners of Climate: Sunlight, Moisture, Temperature, and Wind," www.columbia.edu/itc/cerc/seek/bio2/restrict/modules/module09_content.html

2. J. C. Ryle quoted in *Closer Walk*, vol. 8, November 1990 (Walk Thru the Bible Ministries, Inc.).

3. Chambers, *My Utmost for His Highest*, July 16.

Chapter 10 The Journey of Intimacy

1. Chambers, *My Utmost for His Highest*, May 19.

2. John Piper, "Why Is Satan Left on Earth?" *Desiring God*, May 14, 2003, www.desiringGod.org/library/fresh_words/2003/051403.html.

3. *As Good As It Gets*, DVD, directed by James L. Brooks (Tristar Pictures, 1997).

Chapter 11 The Path of Divine Regression

1. Associated Press, article on AOL news, May 1, 2003.

2. Chambers, *My Utmost for His Highest*, August 28.

3. Hans Christian Andersen, "The Emperor's New Clothes," in *Fritz Andersen's Fairy Tales*, translated by Jean Hershott (New York: Heritage Press, 1942), 83.

Chapter 12 Knowing Whose Child You Are

1. Henri Nouwen, *The Life of the Beloved* (New York: Crossroad Publishing Company, 1992), 28.

2. Henri Nouwen, *Beyond the Mirror* (New York: Crossroad Publishing Company, 1990), 58.

Chapter 13 The Heart of a Father

1. Henri Nouwen, *The Return of the Prodigal Son* (New York: Doubleday, 1992), 120.

2. Ibid., 124.

3. Henri Nouwen, *Walk With Jesus* (Maryknowl, NY: Orbis Books, 1997), 10.

4. Bernard of Clairvaux was a twelfth-century French pastor and theologian. Info taken from the sermon notes of James C. Denison, Park Cities Baptist Church, Dallas, June 16, 2001.

5. Os Guinness, *The Call* (Nashville: Word, 1998), 244.

Dr. Deborah Newman writes weekly devotional articles that are published on her website, www.TeaTimeForYourSoul.com. You can sign up at her website to receive these free weekly email devotionals.

Dr. Deborah Newman can be contacted for speaking engagements at Drdnewman@aol.com.